Murray McBride was born in London and grew up outside the Christian faith, but life changed when he encountered God while farming in Devon. Murray met his future wife Karin when they were both serving at the Lee Abbey community in 1982. He began to learn to communicate the Christian faith to young people as a full-time youth worker in Torquay. He trained as an evangelist with the Church of England's Church Army and, for over ten years, led missions in many parts of the UK, supporting local churches in their outreach to the community. Recognized for his use of creative evangelism, Murray was presented with the Cuthbert Bardsley award. He has written several evangelistic leaflets and is the aut *Lifesavers*. Respond at Trinity Theologic. ordained minister in the Anglican Church. Having worked with several parishes, first in the diocese of Lincoln and then in Carlisle, he is now an army chaplain ministering among soldiers and their familes. Murray drives a 30-year-old MG sports car and loves chocolate, hill-walking, watching movies with Karin and using creativity to share the life-changing message of Jesus with colour, joy and imagination. His first book for BRF, *Walking with Jesus through Advent and Christmas*, was published in September 2005.

Text copyright © Murray McBride 2006
Illustrations copyright © Simon Smith 2006
The author asserts the moral right
to be identified as the author of this work

Published by
The Bible Reading Fellowship
First Floor, Elsfield Hall
15–17 Elsfield Way, Oxford OX2 8FG
Website: www.brf.org.uk

ISBN-10: 1 84101 399 4
ISBN-13: 978 1 84101 399 2

First published 2006
10 9 8 7 6 5 4 3 2 1 0

Acknowledgments
Scripture quotations are taken from the Contemporary English Version of the
Bible published by HarperCollins Publishers, copyright © 1991, 1992, 1995
American Bible Society.

A catalogue record for this book is available from the British Library

Printed in Singapore by Craft Print International Ltd

Living Church

Exploring the Christian Church today

Murray McBride

*To my fellow evangelists in the Church Army
who work with schools.*

To my wife, Karin: thank you.

Contents

foreword

Churches and schools are part of their local community and both work for the good of that community. Local churches have a vital role in supporting and encouraging schools, and church members can become involved in a variety of ways. They can help schools meet their legal requirements to provide a broad and balanced curriculum which promotes the pupils' spiritual, moral, social, cultural, physical, mental and emotional development, and prepares them for the opportunities, responsibilities and experiences of adult life.

An essential ingredient in fulfilling this requirement is the teaching of religious education (RE). RE raises challenging questions about the ultimate meaning and purpose of life, beliefs about God, the self and the nature of reality, issues of right and wrong and what it means to be human. It develops pupils' knowledge and understanding of Christianity, other world faiths and religious traditions as well as other worldviews that offer answers to such questions. It offers opportunities for personal reflection and spiritual development. It enhances pupils' awareness and understanding of religions and beliefs, teachings, practices and forms of expression, along with the influence of religion on individuals, families, communities and cultures.

OFSTED recognizes that people from outside schools play a positive role in primary school RE and stated in a recent report that, where RE has improved, schools have often made closer links with local faith communities. It is clear that if churches can help schools to deliver the requirements of the RE syllabus, all parties benefit: schools are resourced and supported to teach good-quality RE and the church ensures that the teaching of Christianity is grounded in the reality of the local Christian community and a living, relevant and accessible faith.

This book, which is first and foremost practical, includes a variety of ideas for learning about the living church, catering for different learning styles. Many of the resources needed for delivering the activities are also provided. *Living Church* is a gift for busy primary teachers and for churches seeking engagement with their local school.

Margaret Nicholson, Director of Education for the Diocese of Newcastle

Introduction

School trips offer many opportunities for creative learning, but often overlook that treasure house of history, faith and culture available on the doorstep: the local church. The *Living Church* project is designed to unite the local church with its local schools, to unlock the building and the community it represents as an interactive learning resource for children in Years 2–6.

Simply visiting an empty church can be a cold, dim and disappointing study of stones and bones. The *Living Church* project aims to bring the building alive with the sights, sounds, smells and tastes of the living church within its walls. The project provides schools and churches with ready-to-use material for an interactive learning experience in which everyone can take part. The experience brings different parts of the building to life through the dramatic re-enactment of familiar ceremonies such as baptism and marriage; explores physical attributes such as furnishings, architecture, vestments and artefacts; and brings the senses to life with the living tradition of the local Christian faith community, through its music, colour and storytelling.

John's Gospel reminds us that God came in person to live with us: 'The Word became a human being and lived here with us' (John 1:14). The Christian faith does not comprise disembodied concepts, but the living faith of a real community of people who embody their Christian beliefs in everyday life. *Living Church* teaches the Christian faith by allowing religious words to become flesh and blood through the lives of real people. The material enables Christian ceremonies to be brought alive in a way that children can understand and relate to, through the re-enactment of the sacraments and celebrations that are part of church life.

HOW TO USE LIVING CHURCH

Living Church is designed to be used as a teaching experience in small groups, followed by a celebration with the class or year group as a whole. Large groups give a sense of occasion, while smaller learning groups give pupils a greater opportunity to ask questions.

The material is written in the form of short storyteller's teaching scripts. This enables the local minister to give an overall welcome to the group as a whole and then to divide the children into smaller groups, each with an adult leader—either a teacher or a volunteer from the church. The groups go to different parts of the church, where teachers and church members use the storyteller's scripts to bring the building alive through different activities. Ideally, each adult should be allocated one storytelling script, with the small learning groups hearing each story script as they rotate to different areas of the church. The number of options depends on how many storytellers you have available (drawn from both the church and the school) and how many topics you wish to cover. Ideally, the storytellers should learn their script or familiarize themselves with the material enough to put the teaching into their own words. Once each small group has visited each learning area, the children then reunite to experience a big celebration, such as the re-enactment of a wedding, ideally led by the minister.

Each topic also includes learning quote cards to help the children distil what they have learnt about the session, and storyboard cards, which are designed to be used as flash cards during the storytelling, or as part of a project file to remind children of different aspects of their learning. There are also several activity sheets that can be added to the project files or used on the day. Even if you are not planning to build up a project file, the storyboards will provide a good illustration for the small groups to show what the re-enactments might look like and help the children understand the different aspects of living worship.

The *Living Church* project offers no more than a brief encounter: there will not be enough time to explore individual topics in great depth. You will therefore find it helpful to appoint a timekeeper to alert the storytellers when it is time to complete their presentation and move a group on to the next storyteller. Poor timekeeping will mean that you run short of time in the final stages. Note: Suggested time allocations are given within individual teaching scripts.

An RE resource for teachers

Living Church has been designed as a ready-to-use resource for teachers working with children in Years 2–6. With reference to the Non-statutory National

Framework for Religious Education, the material covers many of the learning attainments required for teaching Christianity by making use of local resources such as the Christian faith community, the church building, sacred writings, artefacts and traditions from the worldwide Church. The strength of *Living Church* is its experiential approach to exploring religion. The material offers schools the means to experience a wide range of worship, sacraments and celebrations, and provides the space to help children consider feelings of wonder, praise, thanks and sadness.

Cross-curricular studies

As well as covering many of the learning attainments for the Non-statutory National Framework for Religious Education, the *Living Church* project offers an ideal opportunity to use religious education as a point of contact for curricular studies in English, art, history, technology, music and geography.

The Christian community

Equally, *Living Church* encourages the Christian community to offer itself as a resource for schools. In bringing the local church building to life with music, ritual and colour, pupils have the opportunity to explore the meaning and purpose that faith inspires in the daily lives of local Christians.

Role play
The use of role play to explore celebrations such as baptism and marriage enables children to understand more readily the challenges of religious belief, commitment, society and belonging to a community. Role play creates an enjoyable means for children to participate fully using their imagination, while at the same time enabling them to realize that they are playing characters and are not personally involved.

Pupils are invited to take on the roles of characters in two imaginary families, to explore how these families take part in different aspects of the church's life. Their lives are followed through different worship services, with opportunities to stop and think about how their character might feel and how the building, music and celebrations help to give meaning and purpose to life.

As well as introducing the theme of beliefs and lifestyle, *Living Church* also introduces the idea of a sacred space within a community. Visiting a church can be a refreshing discovery of sacredness in a busy and impersonal world. It is a great privilege for the church community to be welcoming guardians of holy ground: an oasis of peace and security at the heart of society. The *Living Church* project seeks to share this sacred space with children who may never have visited a holy place or experienced the timelessness of the spiritual dimension. Visiting a place of Christian worship also enables children to experience the sacred books, songs and space of the faith community, together with the sacredness of each person.

NB: The material in this book was devised within the Anglican tradition and field-tested with local schools in a parish church. Therefore, many of the terms used are Anglican, although terms and titles have been varied where possible to encompass other Christian denominations. If the minister needs to change terminology to match his or her own denomination, it should be easy to do so—and will provide a point of learning to explain the variety within the Christian Church.

PART
ONE

Getting started

Preparing for the Living Church project

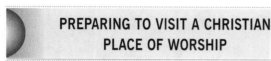

PREPARING TO VISIT A CHRISTIAN PLACE OF WORSHIP

Stage 1: Enlisting help

The school may wish to consider inviting parents to support the *Living Church* project, especially in helping with the journey to and from the church building. Alongside classroom assistants and ancillary staff, parents may also be able to help lead small learning groups. The minister of the church may wish to ask for volunteers from the church's community, especially organists, churchwardens and other key people who understand how the building is used and can be available for the children to ask questions about how the Christian faith affects daily life.

NB: To comply with current legislation, you will need confirmation from the minister of the church that members of the church volunteering to take part in the project hold an Enhanced Certificate of Disclosure from the Criminal Records Bureau. You will also need to ensure that volunteers taking part on the school's behalf also hold such a certificate. Visit www.crb.gov.uk for further information.

Stage 2: Setting the scene

On page 51 you will find a simple timeline showing how the Christian community grew from a group of persecuted followers of Jesus, meeting secretly in homes, into an institutional state religion with public places of worship. The *Living Church* construction model on pages 52–54 shows the development and changes that have taken place in the typical Anglican parish church over the last thousand years, from simple chapels into the complex and multi-faceted buildings that we see today.

Stage 3: Choosing topics of study

Living Church provides a wide range of topics that may be studied during a visit to the local church. Teachers are encouraged to select units according to time restraints and teaching requirements. Please refer to the Contents page for a full list of topics and activities available. A helpful 'jargon buster' glossary of terms can be found on pages 77–80.

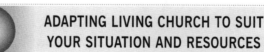

ADAPTING LIVING CHURCH TO SUIT YOUR SITUATION AND RESOURCES

The material in this book is best suited for children in Years 2–6, and the ideal way to organize the project is to plan a *Living Church* day, which will enable pupils to learn about many aspects of church life and worship in a single experience. In this way, teachers can work together for a special RE day involving everything from just one class to year groups, Key Stage groups, or even the whole school. This model is often adopted for activity days in cathedrals around the country.

However, this ideal is not always possible. The material can therefore be split into several learning units, which can be adapted in a pick-and-mix fashion to suit the teaching plan for the year. The project can then be organized into several visits with a group of classes visiting together, or one class visiting on its own. Your choice may therefore be:

✤ One day visit, with several groups and several storytellers.
✤ Two or three short visits, with several groups and several storytellers.
✤ For those with few resources, the material can be adapted to use with one class group and one storyteller. However, this will be second best to the teaching advantages of learning in small groups.

NB: If transport and helpers are a concern, the single-day event will be the easiest to organize.

PREPARING THE SCHOOL

Making contact with the local church minister

If you don't have regular contact with the minister of your local church, the local telephone directory should list his or her number (or the number of the church office) under the name of the church. Ask for a meeting to explore the *Living Church* material together and to establish the level of support available. It is advisable to plan a term ahead in order to give time for everything to be arranged for your visit.

Making use of collective worship

You may wish to consider inviting the local minister or another member of the church to lead an assembly in order to introduce the planned visit to the church. The minister may also be able to advise on the choice of music or songs for the assembly.

Using the construction model preparation session

Living Church introduces the church as a building in the community where special occasions are celebrated. Making the construction model on pages 52–54 will help the children to prepare themselves for their visit to an unfamiliar building.

Preparing for the role play scenarios

For the role play scenarios, you will need to divide the children into mixed groups, with boys and girls in each group. Invite the children to bring along dressing-up clothes to suit the roles they will be playing. You will also need specific items for individual celebrations, such as large dolls or special clothes for a baptism, and jackets, waistcoats, ties, shirts, a wedding dress, a veil, a bunch of flowers and hats for a wedding.

Recruiting adult support

Classroom assistants, parents and members of the church community will be needed to stay with each small group as they rotate from one area of the church to another. As previously stated, all adult helpers will need to have an Enhanced Certificate of Disclosure from the Criminal Records Bureau (CRB). Visit www.crb.gov.uk or www.disclosure.gov.uk for further details.

Safety first

It is advisable to visit the church with the minister beforehand to assess where groups can gather and to identify any possible dangers, such as uneven steps or flagstones. If the children are walking to the church, it is advisable for a member of staff to walk the route beforehand to identify the safest crossings. School guidelines on health and safety should be observed at all times during the visit.

Photographs

A photographic record of the visit would greatly enhance a *Living Church* classroom display. You will need to seek permission from the children's parents or guardians and allocate someone in the class to take group photographs of the activities.

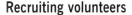

PREPARING THE CHURCH COMMUNITY

Recruiting volunteers

The minister is the key contact with the church and will be able to advise you on who to invite to be involved in the project. Volunteers will need to be able to use the storytelling scripts and answer the children's questions about the faith community. Those to approach could include churchwardens, musicians, lay ministers and members with experience of uniformed organizations and church-based children's work.

Preparing the church building

Having everything prepared ahead of the visit, so that artefacts are ready to use, will ensure that the activities run smoothly and keep to time. You will need to produce A4 signs to label items such as the font, pulpit, Communion table, lectern and so on. The minister will be able to give advice to help you. The following areas of the church will need to be prepared in advance:

❖ The font (water, oil, candle and candle lighter)
❖ The pews or chairs (kneelers, Bibles, hymn books, service books and welcome cards)
❖ The pulpit (Bible)
❖ The altar or Communion table (candles, cloths, chalice, paten, candle lighter, blackcurrant juice, bread)
❖ The organ (music edition hymn books, clear access)
❖ The choir stalls (choir robes, crucifer's processional cross, processional candles, candle holders)
❖ The vestry (vestments, service register)

Follow-up

The minister may wish to find out whether project work can be borrowed to display in the church after the visit. You may also wish to explore any other way in which the Christian community could offer the building or the skills of their people as a resource for the school.

Advertising the event in the church community

The minister may wish to put a notice about the event in the church newsletter or weekly notice sheet, or display a poster. Details need to include the date and time of the planned visit, plus information about the event. For example, 'We are planning a joint project uniting our church with *(name of the local school)* as partners in learning. This initiative, called *Living Church*, is an educational day to help the school learn more about the Christian faith. If you would like to offer practical support for the day, please contact *(name and telephone number of minister)*. You will need to hold an Enhanced Certificate of Disclosure from the Criminal Records Bureau and be willing to be questioned by the schoolchildren about your faith and the life of the church.'

◖ A CREATIVE PREPARATION SESSION ◗

This preparation session takes place in the classroom before the visit to the church. The session should last approximately 30 minutes.

You will need:
- ✪ Pictures of typical church buildings
- ✪ One copy of the *Living Church* timeline on page 51
- ✪ Copies of the *Living Church* construction model on pages 52–54, photocopied on to thin card (one model per child)
- ✪ One copy of the brief history of the *Living Church* information sheet on page 55
- ✪ Copies of the *Living Church* poster on page 56 (one poster per child or as required: see page 15 for suggested use)
- ✪ Scissors
- ✪ Colouring materials
- ✪ Glue

In preparation for the session, gather together pictures of typical church buildings and photocopy the *Living Church* timeline on page 51. Also, cut out and assemble a demonstration construction model from pages 52–54, but don't join all three parts together at this point. Keep the tower, nave and chancel separate from each other.

Introduce the idea of *Living Church* to the children by saying that you are going to have a special project to explore why there is a church in your community, and that you will be going on a special trip to meet the minister and discover more about what Christians believe. Show a picture of a typical church (the local church, if possible). Ask if anyone knows what the building is called. Ask if anyone has ever been in a church. What happened when they visited a church? Ask if anyone knows what special things might happen in a church building.

The Living Church timeline

The account below gives a very brief history of how the local church developed over a long period of time. It is intended to be used in conjunction with the *Living Church* timeline.

Explain that we need to go a long way back in time to find the beginnings of Christianity and the Christian church. Display the *Living Church* timeline so that everyone can see it. The timeline shows how the Christian community grew from meetings held secretly in each other's homes immediately after the death and resurrection of Jesus, into an institutionalized state religion with public church buildings, steeped in history and tradition.

Take the class through the different stages of the timeline, stopping along the way to answer any questions that might arise. Explain that AD is short for the Latin *Anno Domini*, which means 'In the year of our Lord'. The life of Jesus has had such a remarkable effect on the world that it was decided to begin numbering our years from the date of Jesus' birth. This indicates just how unique in history Jesus was.

AD1–30

AD1 is the estimated birth date of Jesus. Jesus was born in Bethlehem, in modern-day Israel. The Bible tells us that Jesus began his adult work of teaching people about God when he was about 30 years old (about AD30).

Jesus was not trained as a religious leader. He did not have a temple or building where people could gather to listen to him teaching about God. Sometimes he taught in the local synagogues (the religious buildings of the Jewish community), sometimes he taught in the open air and sometimes he taught in people's homes. As well as telling people stories to help them understand about God, he also spent time praying and healing those who were unwell.

After Jesus died and rose again, his closest followers

met together in each other's homes because there were no church buildings. As the community of Christians grew, it was the people themselves who were the 'church', in that they were the worshipping community of people who followed Jesus Christ. Today, it is still the faith community, rather than the building, that is the real church. It is for that reason that this project is called *Living Church*. The foundations of the worldwide Church of Jesus started with the living faith of people who believed in Jesus, rather than in the dead stones used to make a building.

AD33–40

About AD33, the religious authorities of the day began to feel threatened by Jesus because of his popularity with everyday people and the unconventional message of his teaching. He was turning people's understanding of God upside down, and thousands of people had begun to follow him. Jesus knew that he was unpopular with the religious leaders, but he continued to teach about God. Finally, he was put on trial and executed on a cross. He had done nothing wrong, other than threaten the stability of those who thought they knew what religion was all about. But then something extraordinary happened: three days after his death, the stone tomb where Jesus had been buried was found to be empty—even though a heavy stone had been rolled across the entrance. Jesus had risen from the dead. In the next few weeks, many people reported seeing him, and the Bible tells us how he met with his close friends and continued to teach and encourage them for 40 days before returning to heaven and sending his Holy Spirit into the world to lead his followers. It was these close friends of Jesus who were given the task of building the Christian Church.

After Jesus' return to heaven, his followers met in the Jewish temple in Jerusalem to continue worshipping God—but this time as Christians rather than as Jews. It wasn't long before the religious leaders began to see the followers of Jesus as a serious threat because their numbers were growing so fast, so they banned them from using the great temple in Jerusalem.

By AD34, the followers of Jesus had become known as Christians. The Jewish authorities hoped that the newfound Christian faith might dwindle away to nothing, but, instead, the number of Christians grew—so much so that the authorities began a policy of hunting them down and either putting them in prison or putting them to death. At that time, there was no legal protection from this persecution, so Christians met in secret in their homes to worship God through prayer, singing, sharing bread and wine and learning more about Jesus. They also started using secret signs to identify themselves, and many moved away from Jerusalem to escape being killed.

One of the religious leaders was a man called Saul of Tarsus. Saul led many attacks on the early Christians. One day, when he was on his way to Damascus to hunt out and imprison Christians in that town, he met the resurrected Jesus on the road between Jerusalem and Damascus. The experience had such a marked effect on him that he became an ardent follower of Jesus, changing his name from Saul to Paul. Today, he is often known as St Paul. He travelled great distances on foot and by boat in order to tell people about Jesus. He started many new churches in the countries surrounding the eastern Mediterranean, teaching about Jesus both in synagogues and in people's homes. Much of the New Testament part of the Bible is made up of letters written by St Paul to the churches he established.

AD40–330

In the final part of the first century AD, the followers of Jesus became a regular target for persecution by local leaders, kings and Roman emperors—most famously by Nero, who blamed the burning of Rome on the Christians. In some countries, however, things remained quiet and the church continued to grow, but even in these places waves of persecution would force many to meet together in secret places.

AD330

In the year 330, Emperor Constantine was converted to Christianity and ended 300 years of persecution for the Christian communities. Eventually, the emperor decided that the Christian religion would become the one official religion of the Roman empire. Many Roman temples were reused, clearing away previous religious artefacts and worship, and were converted to be used for Christian worship with new symbols, statues, celebrations and rituals.

AD400

Christianity was introduced to Britain over a very long period of time, in the first instance by traders, settlers, soldiers and government workers and later by Christians who lived in religious communities abroad. These communities sent missionaries from Rome and Ireland to establish Britain's first Christian churches with their own locally designed church buildings. The missionaries would persuade a local king or landowner to pay for the building of a simple wooden or stone barn construction. The church was used for worship, but it was also often the biggest public building in which ordinary people could gather. The buildings had no seats, which meant that they were suitable for a range of events, such as village meetings, parties and markets. This area was the hub of community activity, including worship, and became known as the nave, or public part. The word comes from the Latin *navis*, which means a ship. The ceiling of the nave is arched, forming the shape of an upturned boat.

AD900

During the tenth century, towers were added to many churches. Sometimes bells were hung from the top. The bells were used to mark the time, to call people to worship and to celebrate events such as weddings. In times of danger, the bells would ring out to warn people of attack. The towers were built strong and high so that people could hide from the invaders who often raided British towns and villages. The church building became a sanctuary in times of danger.

AD1200

By the 13th century, religion had developed far beyond the 'house church' format so familiar to first-century Christians. Twelve hundred years later, the service, led by a priest, was carried out in Latin—so ordinary people would not have understood a word. This division between priest and people was emphasized even more with the building of a chancel to the east end of the public nave. The chancel contained the high altar and seats for the clergy. The nave was separated from the chancel by a latticework screen, often with a crucifix on top. This screen was known as the rood screen. (The word 'rood' comes from the old English word for a cross.) The screen kept people out of the chancel and prevented them from being part of the worship. It was a private place kept especially for praying, singing and celebrating special services, led by priests or monks.

AD1534

In 1534, King Henry VIII proclaimed himself to be head of the Church of England. He took control of the churches away from the pope in Rome and began to loot cathedrals and churches for their precious treasures, with the excuse that they were too ornamental and too much in the Roman tradition. One positive result of Henry VIII's actions was that church services started to be conducted in English rather than Latin, so that ordinary people could understand what was being said.

AD1548

During the reign of the child king, Edward VI, the king's council ordered churches to be stripped of all things 'corrupt, vain and superstitious', which empowered people to tear down statues, pull down chancel screens and whitewash religious murals. The stone altars in the chancels were smashed and replaced with wooden tables. A dramatic change was that these new altars were brought forward into the nave for people to stand around while celebrating Communion.

If you look carefully in many older churches, you will see signs of what was destroyed during this time.

AD1553

When King Edward died at the age of 15, Queen Mary took the throne. The new queen wanted to restore churches to their pre-Reformation days. Her plans to marry Philip II of Spain enraged many English people who feared being controlled by Spain, their old enemy. This fear began a rebellion that spread throughout the land. In response, Mary ordered the execution of hundreds of those who rebelled. Many were burnt at the stake, among them priests, bishops and scholars. When Mary died, her half-sister, Queen Elizabeth I, came to the throne and began the tradition of ordering every parish church to display the royal coat of arms prominently as a reminder of who controlled the Church in England.

AD1642

In 1642, a struggle between the king (Charles I) and government led to a bitter civil war, known as the English Civil War. This war was not just about power; it also involved a large element of religious conflict because people felt passionately about their religion. The government troops were influenced by a Bible-based line of Christianity called Puritanism. The Puritans saw the remnants of Catholic rituals and outward symbols as dangerous idols that confused people and prevented them from following Jesus in the ways set out in the Bible. As a result, government troops felt duty-bound to destroy any statues, artwork or symbols that they believed were distracting people from focusing on God's holy Bible. Many old churches show the damage caused as a result of this struggle to win people's minds.

AD1660–1666

Following the English Civil War, Charles I was eventually beheaded and the Commonwealth established. When Charles II was restored to the throne in 1660, the bishops, the Prayer Book and the Anglican system were all re-established. During this time (in 1666), a great fire broke out in London, destroying 84 ancient parish churches in the capital. Christopher Wren was chosen to design a new kind of church, radically different from the ancient kind, expressing a new way of thinking. The style was called Baroque. It was theatrical and modelled itself on the classical temples of Greece of 1000BC. Wren began a new fashion of building churches, which were bright, with a classical look inside.

AD1818

When the Industrial Revolution started to draw the population in from the countryside, cities began to grow, but there were few churches. Parliament responded in 1818 with *The Church Buildings Act*, offering grants totalling one million pounds to build over 200 new churches in the industrial areas. This began the greatest period of church building since the Norman Conquest. The classic simplicity of the buildings gave way to Victorian Gothic, imitating the medieval style of tall pointed arches, with elaborately decorated woodcarvings. Stained glass and masonry work revived skills used in medieval churches. There was also a revival of medieval symbols, religious clothing and a more elaborate pre-Reformation style of worship influenced by the Roman Catholic tradition. Some people think that the Gothic style of churches in the cities, with their tall spires and rich ornamentation, was intended to challenge the drab, functional factories and workers' tenements, and that the priests' colourful vestments and dramatic styles of worship were intended to challenge the functional attitudes of the Industrial Revolution with an exciting spiritual view of the world that would win people back to the life of the church.

The 20th century and beyond

Since the beginning of the 20th century, a variety of styles has been used when building new churches. Many are multi-purpose buildings, similar to the idea of the early Saxon churches, which can be used for midweek meetings of community groups and be converted into a place of worship for the congregation. Some congregations meet in schools and in people's homes for worship, taking us back full circle to the beginning of the Christian community.

I wonder if you can guess how old your local church is. Where do you think it fits into our history timeline? The church buildings that we see today might have changed a great deal, both outside and inside, since they were first built. While taking part in the *Living Church* project, you can look out for signs of these changes. The changes give us clues to events that were taking place over the course of history, and show how Christians have kept some important things the same but changed other things over the centuries.

The Living Church construction model

The church building construction model shows the development and changes that have typically taken place in church design over the last 1500 years, changing from simple chapels into the complex and fascinating buildings we see today.

Give a construction model to each child in the class. Then show the children the one that you have already made. First of all, explain how the early church meant the people, not the building—using the 'Brief history

of the *Living Church*' information sheet, photocopied from page 55. Next, show the simple nave building that was introduced in AD400, once again referring to the information sheet. Then show how towers were added around AD900, referring again to the information sheet as you do so. Finally, show how the chancel was built on to the nave from around AD1200, once again referring to the information sheet.

Finally, invite the children to make up their *Living Church* models. Use the information sheet to recap the development of the church design as the children make up the models, starting with the nave. When the models have all been made, they can be used to form a classroom display as part of the *Living Church* project.

The Living Church poster

The *Living Church* poster can be used in a variety of ways during the learning process. For example, it can form part of the creative preparation session before the visit, it can be used as a means of information for the staff and helpers in preparation for the project or on the day of the visit, or the children can use it during the visit itself. It can also be used as part of the classroom display after the visit.

The poster can be found on page 56. When you have decided how you wish to use it, photocopy the number of copies required and supply colouring materials if it is to be used as a colouring-in activity with the children. Below is a fuller list of suggested ways in which the poster may be used:

✤ To illustrate the inside of a church building to the group before a visit.
✤ To help the teacher gain a working understanding of the layout of a typical church.
✤ To illustrate where the storytellers can best lead different re-enactments.
✤ To point out various architectural features which are special to churches.
✤ To help the group understand where they are inside a large church when they are involved in an activity that is specifically located in a part of the building designed for that purpose.
✤ To use as a map for teachers during the day if several activity groups are working at the same time.
✤ To show the direction and progression of groups as they move from one location and activity to another.
✤ To use as part of a classroom display after the church visit.

Before the visit, it is advisable to photocopy the 'Religious language jargon buster' (glossary of terms) on pages 77–80 as a reference for teachers and their helpers.

9.30 am	Arrive at church. Minister welcomes everyone in one large group. 1. Introduction to the day
9.45 am	2. Three small learning groups (rotating after 15 minutes): a) Living worship: Baptism b) Living worship: The Bible c) Living worship: Prayer
10.30 am	3. Refreshments
10.45 am	4. Design your own church activity sheet (in small learning groups)
11.00 am	5. Living worship: Holy Communion (all together)
11.30 am	6. Three small learning groups (rotating after 15 minutes) a) Living worship: the Christian calendar b) Living worship: Music c) Living worship: Vestments
12.15 pm	7. **LUNCH BREAK**
12.30 pm	8. Three small learning groups (rotating after 15 minutes) a) Living worship: Funeral b) The living churchyard c) Living worship: the worldwide Church
1.15 pm	9. Living worship: Marriage (all together)
2.00 pm	10. Question time and a brief act of worship (Bible reading, song and Lord's Prayer)
2.30 pm	11. Depart

The Living Church
activity sessions

Welcome and introduction to the day

Preparation

 You will need:

❋ A completed *Living Church* construction model

Remind small group storytellers to prepare their areas of the church so that they can begin working with their small groups as soon as the overall introduction has been completed. Have a finished *Living Church* construction model ready to show the children.

Teaching area

Gather the children by the main church door.

Aim

To welcome the children and help them to get their bearings in the building.

Action

Divide the class into three groups of equal size. It is helpful if the groups can be prearranged, with a mixture of boys and girls (if possible) in each group. These learning groups will rotate after each 15-minute session, so that all groups experience all storytelling spaces.

Time allocation

 10 minutes

Learning quote cards

On page 57, you will find cards to help the children reflect on the experience of each topic they complete. You will need to photocopy one card per session for each child taking part. Simply ask the children to pause at the end of each activity, reflect on their learning experience and write a short sentence on their card. The cards can then be added to their project file or collected for a classroom display.

Storyboard cards

The storyboard cards are designed to be used as flash cards as the storytelling progresses, or as memory cards for the children to help them to recall each stage of the storytelling or re-enactment. The cards can be photocopied so that each child has his or her own set to add to the project file, or just one set of each storyboard can be photocopied for the classroom display. The children can colour the cards in as desired.

 STORYTELLER'S SCRIPT

Welcome to *(name of church)*. What special things do you think take place in this building?

This church is known as 'the house of God' because local people come here to meet with God. Look how big the doors are! This reminds us of the big welcome everyone receives. Everyone is invited to come and meet with God in this place. A church is not a club. It is a place where everyone— whoever they are, whatever their background, colour, race or religion—is welcome. No one is excluded.

Can you remember the name of this church?

Perhaps the church has a patron saint or a special name. Talk about the name of the church and why it might be called by that name. The following script is an example.

This church is called 'St Peter's Church', which means that St Peter is the 'patron saint' of this church. St Peter was a fisherman who became a very close friend of Jesus. His name reminds us that this church only exists because people like Peter listened to Jesus and followed his teaching. Peter passed his belief that Jesus is the Son of God to others, and those people have passed on the Christian message, down through the generations and so to us today.

Look around you. Can you see a window, a picture or sign that commemorates the life of the patron saint of this church? See how many other names you can find in this church today. All these people have followed Jesus' teaching in their daily life.

Hold up the Living Church construction model.

Now we are inside the church building, we can see the different parts of a church. Think back to when we made our *Living Church* construction models. Can you remember which part of the church was built first? The nave is the main part of the church building. It is the most public part—the part where the congregation sits. The tower was the next part to be added. It was built so that the people could find protection in times of trouble. Bells were hung in the tower to warn the people of danger, to mark time and to call the people to the church for worship. Lastly, the chancel was added to create a more private area. This area is sometimes called the sanctuary. It is where the altar or Communion table may be found.

Today we are going to find out what happens in all three areas of the church building—the nave, the tower and the chancel. The word 'church' doesn't only mean the building itself. The word 'church' also refers to the people who meet within the house of God. They can't all be here today, so

we are going to imagine that we are the people who belong to this church.

First of all, this morning, we are going to act out what happens when a baptism takes place. Then, we are going to find out how the people who worship at this church use the holy Bible and why they pray to God. Next we are going to find out what happens at a service of Holy Communion, think about the pattern of the Christian year and learn about the way God can be praised through music and singing. Finally, just before lunch, we are going to find out about the special clothes that ministers wear in church. After lunch, we are going to find out what happens outside the church and in what ways the people who worship here care about the whole world and share their faith far beyond the walls of this building.

Because we are going to be acting, each of us will be invited to think up a new name for ourselves as we go along, so that we can act out each part of our drama and see how this building can be changed from cold stones to a living church.

Preparing the learning groups

Divide the children into three learning groups as previously planned. Invite each group to choose a name so that you can identify each one. Choosing one of the names of Jesus' closest friends would be suitable: for example, Mary, Peter, John, Martha, Andrew, James, Philip, Joanna, Bartholomew, Thomas, Matthew, James, Thaddeus or Simon. Make sure that each child knows which name has been chosen for his or her group.

Invite the first three storytellers to lead their small group into the different parts of the church building. In their groups, the children will learn simultaneously, rotating to the next storyteller after 15 minutes until every group has experienced all of the first three storytelling areas.

When the point in the programme is reached for the next three storytelling areas, you may either use the same three storytellers or three further storytellers, depending on the number of helpers you have. The same principle will apply with the final three story-telling activities, which take place in the afternoon.

Living worship: Baptism

Preparation

 You will need:

- Baby dolls
- Water
- A jug
- The church's large paschal (Easter) candle
- A small candle
- A candle lighter or matches
- Baptism storyboard card photocopied from page 58 (one per child if they are building a project file)
- Learning quote cards photocopied from page 57 (one per child)

The baptism storyboard card can be found on page 58. Set everything up near the baptism font before the session starts. Put water into the jug and fill the font from the jug.

Teaching area
The font.

Aim
To discover that baptism marks the beginning of the Christian journey of faith. Explain that we are going to re-enact the baptism of an imaginary child (a doll) from an imaginary family (role play).

Action
Gather around the font and the paschal candle.

Time allocation

 15 minutes

 STORYTELLER'S SCRIPT

Does anyone know what this is called? It is called a font. Can you guess what the font is made of? Put your hand on the font to feel the material it is made of. Do you know what special purpose the font has in the church? The font is used to baptize people of all ages, from tiny babies, just a few weeks old, to elderly people perhaps 100 years old! Sometimes you may hear people refer to a baptism as a 'christening', but the church normally uses the name 'baptism', because this is the name given in the Bible. (You can find the story of John the Baptist and Jesus' baptism in Matthew 3:1–17.)

Baptism services take many different forms depending on what type of Christian tradition and country the people are from. However, all baptisms are a service of welcome into the worldwide Church of Jesus Christ. When a small child is baptized, adults make promises to bring that child up to know and follow Jesus. Adults who are baptized make promises to follow Jesus, in their own words, thoughts and actions. This is the beginning of a lifelong journey that will help each person to follow Jesus more closely.

To re-enact a service of baptism, choose two children from your group to be the parents of the child being baptized. Give them a doll. Ask them to make up a first name for themselves and a surname for their role-play family. Ask the mum and dad what name they would like to choose for their 'baby'. Next, choose three children to be the baby's godparents. (Traditionally, two of the godparents are the same sex as the child.) If there are enough children in the group to make a second family unit, repeat as above, and so on, until all the children in the group have a role. If there are not enough children in the group to make up further family units, the remaining children can become the 'congregation'.

What do you think a godparent's job is? Godparents are people who are followers of Jesus. The baby's godparents promise at the baptism service to help the baby learn more about following Jesus as he or she grows up. The child's learning might include reading about Jesus in the Bible, going to church and praying.

The form of baptism service used below is a simplified version of the baptism service from the Church of England's Common Worship *liturgy. This is only role play, so if a minister is not available the storyteller can take their place and read their part.*

Minister's introduction to the congregation

Minister: Today we welcome this child (these children) into the church of Jesus Christ. This child (these children) need(s) the help of his/her (their) parents and godparents to grow up as a follower (followers) of Jesus.

The promises of parents and godparents

Parents and godparents stand.

Minister: The church asks parents and godparents to make these baptism promises… Will you turn away from doing wrong?
Parents and godparents: With the help of God we will.
Minister: Will you turn to Jesus for help?
Parents and godparents: With the help of God we will.
Minister: Will you follow Jesus all your life?'
Parents and godparents: With the help of God we will.

The sign of the cross

Minister: *(Baby's name)*, I mark you with the sign of the cross, the sign of Christ.

Minister makes the sign of the cross on the forehead of the child/doll.

The sign of the water

Minister: *(Baby's name)*, I baptize you in the name of the Father, Son and Holy Spirit.

When baptizing a child, it is customary to pour a handful of water on the forehead of the child. With adults, in many traditions the person being baptized will go into a baptism pool, a river or the sea where they will be completely immersed under the water for a moment.

The sign of light

Light the large paschal (Easter) candle. Light the small candle from the large paschal candle.

Minister: This is a sign to remind us that Jesus is called the light for the world. All who follow Jesus are promised that, when they feel lost and in the dark, Jesus will give them the light of hope to live by and overcome the darkness of doubt and fear. *(Turning to the child)* You have received the light of Christ; walk in this light all your life.

Give the lit candle to the parents. For safety reasons you may prefer to light a small candle on a stand near the children. Repeat the baptism liturgy with the other family groups as appropriate.

——— ◆ ———

Follow-up

Give each child a learning quote card and ask them to write a sentence on the card about their learning experience during the baptism re-enactment. The cards can be used later to build a folder or illustrate a school display in the classroom.

Finish by asking if there are any questions. When the group is ready, direct them to the next storytelling area.

Living worship: the Bible

Preparation

You will need:

- A selection of Bibles
- The Bible storyboard card photocopied from page 59 (one per child if they are building a project folder)
- Learning quote cards photocopied from page 57 (one per child)

Have a selection of Bibles available for the children to look at as appropriate during the storytelling period.

Teaching area

The chairs or pews nearest to the lectern, followed by the area around the pulpit.

Aim

To discover how important the Bible is for Christians and why it is often referred to as 'the word of God'. Christians believe that the Bible reveals what God is like, teaches people how best to live, bears witness to the life of Jesus Christ, the Son of God, and helps people to follow Jesus in their daily lives.

Action

If there is a special stand for the Bible (a lectern), gather the learning group around it. In some churches, the lectern may be shaped as an eagle; in others the lectern may be of a simple wooden design.

Time allocation

 15 minutes

STORYTELLER'S SCRIPT

Every Christian church places special importance on its holy book. Do you know what this book is called? The Bible is common to the faith of all Christians in every part of the world. It has been translated into many languages.

The Bible contains many famous sayings, some of which are used even today in everyday conversation. People don't always realize that the saying they are using comes from the Bible! For example, people say that they will 'turn the other cheek' when they don't want to argue with someone else. This phrase comes from Jesus' teaching about not trying to get even with anyone (Matthew 5:38–39). Another famous saying from the Bible is 'Love others as much as you love yourself.' This saying sums up what Jesus taught about the way we should treat each other (Luke 10:25–37).

Here are four of the most popular questions asked by children about the Bible.

Who wrote the Bible? The word 'Bible' gives us a clue. It comes from the ancient Greek word *biblia*, which means 'books'. The Bible may look like one book, but it is actually 66 books, all together under one cover. Many of the books of the Bible are named after the person who wrote that part of the Bible. There are more than 40 different writers in total. Their books were chosen to be in the Bible because it was believed that their work was special—inspired by God.

There are two main parts to the Bible: the Old Testament and the New Testament. The Old Testament was written many years before Jesus was born, but Christians believe that the writings of the Old Testament point towards Jesus' birth. The New Testament was written after Jesus was born and tells the story of his life, death and resurrection and the beginning of the early church.

One of the people who wrote a large part of the New Testament was a man called Paul. Paul wrote two letters to a friend called Timothy. In the second letter, Paul says to Timothy: 'Everything in the Scriptures is God's Word. All of it is useful for teaching and helping people and for correcting them and showing them how to live' (2 Timothy 3:16). Christians believe that what Paul wrote to Timothy is true. It shows why the Bible is sometimes called 'the word of God'.

How long ago was the Bible written? The books and letters collected together to make up the Bible were written over a period of one thousand years. The most modern writings are letters in the New Testament part of the Bible. These letters are almost two thousand years old. Some of the historical events, stories of kings and battles described in the Old Testament part of the Bible date back to three or four thousand years ago.

What kind of book is the Bible? The Bible is not like the books in the school library, which cover single subjects such as biology, history, cooking or maths. As we have said, the Bible is made up of many books. In fact, it is much more like a mini mobile library, containing 66 books in total. Of those books, 39 were written before Jesus was born, and 27 were written after he was born. The 66 books cover a huge range of different subjects, such as:

❖ **Creation**: writings to explain who created and cares for the world.
❖ **History**: writings that record the family history of God's people, telling of their kings, their conflicts, their adventures and their failures.
❖ **Laws**: writings that set out God's laws for his people to live by. Like school rules, these laws are designed to help keep everyone safe.
❖ **Poems and songs**: the songs in the Bible are called Psalms. They give us help and encouragement, but they also include sorrowful songs, songs of love, songs of worship and songs in praise of God.
❖ **Wisdom**: writings that give wise advice about the difficulties of life.
❖ **Prophecy**: challenging writings from people who

were chosen by God to spread his work and make readers think about the state of their whole nation and the world. They help us to think about the kind of communities we are making in God's world.
❖ **Gospels**: four accounts of the life of Jesus, showing why Christians believe that he was the Son of God.
❖ **Letters**: written to the first Christians to encourage and guide them.
❖ **Stories**: accounts of the adventures of the first Christians as they travelled far and wide to tell everyone the good news about Jesus.

Who is in the Bible? There are many people in the Bible whose names have become famous: Noah, who built the ark; Samson, the strong man; Joseph, with the multi-coloured coat; Jonah, who was swallowed by a whale; and David, who killed the giant Goliath, to name but a few. Of course, there is also Jesus, who Christians believe is the Son of God. The New Testament tells us about the stories he told, the amazing things he did and about his cruel death. Most amazing of all is the story of his coming alive again on the first Easter day.

However, the person who is most mentioned in the Bible is God. The Bible tells us many things about God. It shows us what God likes, what God hates, how creative he is in making the world, how strong yet gentle he is, how wise and mysterious. Most of all, the Bible shows us how loving God is. It shows us how he is always with us and, even though we cannot see him, we can see evidence of his presence in our world and in people around us.

The Bible is usually given a place of great honour in the church building. Sometimes it is a very large book. Sometimes it has a stand of its own from which it is read. It is used to teach people about God. Most of the prayers, songs and words of the services come from the Bible. It is the most important book in the church. The Bible is so important that in many churches the people stand up when the Gospel is read—just as you might stand up when a very important or famous person comes into the room. Some churches use special announcements, as you might when an important person arrives and you want everyone to pay attention. After reading part of the Bible, the reader in church may say, 'This is the word of the Lord' and people reply, 'Thanks be to God.'

The storyteller and children move to gather by the pulpit.

Does anyone know what this is called? It is called a pulpit. What do you think happens here? This is the place where someone with training explains the Bible reading and teaches us to how to follow Jesus today in our daily life. Why do you think it is so high? It is high so that the teacher can be seen and heard by everyone.

Invite someone to come and stand in the pulpit, and ask them how they feel: scared... or important?

Follow-up

After the storytelling is completed, you may wish to use one of the activities suggested below as follow-up:

✪ In two pictures, illustrate a Bible being read from the lectern, and someone explaining what the reading means from the pulpit.
✪ The Bible has been translated into many languages. How many languages can you think of, into which it might be translated?
✪ In medieval times, monks and nuns illustrated the Bible with wonderful pictures to produce 'illuminated Bibles'. Choose a sentence or a verse from the Bible and design your own illuminated page to illustrate the words.

Give each child a learning quote card and ask the children to write a sentence on the card about their learning experience during the storytelling about the Bible. The cards can be used later to build a folder or illustrate a school display in the classroom.

Finish by asking if there are any questions. When the group is ready, direct them to the next storytelling area.

Living worship: Prayer

Preparation

 You will need:
- Some candles
- A candle lighter or box of matches
- Samples of Christian icons
- A Bible
- A cross
- Prayer storyboard card photocopied from page 60 (one per child if they are building a project folder)
- Learning quote cards photocopied from page 57 (one per child)

Teaching area

Near a stained-glass window, or in a side chapel or quiet corner of church.

Aim

To discover that prayer shapes the lives of Christians, not only when they are in church but also in everyday life. Christians talk to God about their plans and problems because they believe that God not only listens, but loves us as his children and wants to help us. Spending time with God in this way is called praying. Praying is an essential part of all acts of worship in a church building.

Action

Gather the children near a stained-glass window, or in a side chapel or quiet corner of church.

Time allocation

 15 minutes

 STORYTELLER'S SCRIPT

A church building is sometimes called 'the house of prayer'. Praying is spending time with God; sometimes we can talk and sometimes listen. By spending time with God in prayer, we get to know, and grow closer to, God.

Let's think about the different ways that we can contact people quickly if we need to talk to them. Praying is like calling God on a telephone: it is a two-way conversation. We can talk and we can listen.

We can talk to God about anything we like, but there are four kinds of prayer conversations that we can have with God, which we remember with the letters P-R-A-Y. The letters stand for:

❖ **P**raise: to say how great we think God is for all that he has done.
❖ **R**epent: to say sorry to God for hurting others or living selfishly.
❖ **A**sk: to ask God to help people who are unwell or who need help in any way.
❖ **Y**ourself: to pray about things that are happening in our own lives and to ask for help in living in the way God wants us to live.

In the Bible, and today in the worldwide Church, there are many ways to use our bodies to pray. The way we use our bodies shows how we are feeling: we may feel sad, happy or sorry when we pray to God. Sometimes we can use our whole body: we can pray standing, sitting, kneeling or even lying face down on the ground.

Invite the children to find a space and try each position in turn, thinking or saying how they feel in each different position.

Sometimes we can pray by using just our hands: we can lift our hands up in the air, we can put our hands together (classic image), we can reach our hands out in front of ourselves, or we can cup our hands in our lap.

Invite the children to try each position in turn, thinking or saying how they feel in each different position.

Sometimes we can pray by using just our eyes: we can pray with our eyes shut, imagining that Jesus is with us, or we can pray with our eyes open, looking at a picture, window, cross or candle.

Invite the children to try each position in turn, thinking or saying how they feel in each different position.

Sometimes we can use prayers that other people have made up, or we can just pray in silence, with no words at all.

Jesus taught his closest friends a way of praying that helps us to pray about lots of things that God wants us to talk to him about. Jesus' prayer is called 'The Lord's Prayer'. It is a very famous prayer. Using a famous prayer can sometimes help us when we don't know how to pray. Let's listen to the Lord's Prayer and see if we can spot the different things we are praying about in the prayer. In the Bible, we can find Jesus' prayer in Matthew 6:9–13 and in Luke 11:2–4. In church today, we may say the words of the prayer in modern English:

Our Father in heaven, hallowed be your name,
your kingdom come, your will be done
on earth as in heaven.
Give us today our daily bread.
Forgive us our sins as we forgive those
who sin against us.
Lead us not into temptation but deliver us from evil.
For the kingdom, the power and the glory are yours
now and for ever. Amen.

Sometimes we may say the words in old English:

Our Father who art in heaven, hallowed be thy name,
thy kingdom come, thy will be done,
on earth as it is in heaven.
Give us this day our daily bread.
Forgive us our trespasses

as we forgive those who trespass against us.
And lead us not into temptation
but deliver us from evil.
For thine is the kingdom, the power and the glory
forever and ever. Amen.

Sometimes, however, we may feel that we don't want to say anything at all in prayer. We may just want to come close to God. It's a bit like when you just want to lean on the person who cares for you—your mum or your dad, or your granny. When you lean on someone, you can hear their heartbeat and know that they are with you.

Invite the children to find a space, rest their body in whatever position they choose and simply be quiet for half a minute.

Sometimes, praying can be difficult because it needs us to use our imagination—and it's hard to imagine God, who is invisible. So some Christian churches use things like candles, crosses, stained-glass windows, banners, icons, paintings, Bibles or statues to help people use their imagination to start talking with God. It is important to remember that Christians are not worshipping these objects. It's a bit like looking at a photograph of someone you love: you don't love the photo itself—it is just paper! You love the person in the photo. In the same way, Christians don't worship crosses or other symbols. These things simply help people to remember Jesus when they pray.

Invite the children to sit quietly with a cross, a Bible, an icon or a lighted candle. Which one of these objects helps them most to think about God?

——— ✦ ———

 Follow-up

Give each child a learning quote card and ask the children to write a sentence on the card about their learning experience during the storytelling about prayer. The cards can be used later to build a folder or illustrate a school display in the classroom.

Finish by asking if there are any questions. When the group is ready, direct them to the next storytelling area.

Living worship: Holy Communion

Preparation

 You will need:

- A table
- A white linen tablecloth
- A Bible
- A chalice or earthenware goblet
- A paten or simple earthenware plate
- Candles
- A candle lighter or box of matches
- A cross
- Bread
- Fruit juice in an earthenware jug
- Disposable cups for all the children
- Holy Communion storyboard card photocopied from page 61 (one per child if they are building a project folder)
- Learning quote cards photocopied from page 57 (one per child)

If you are not able to use the altar or Communion table in the church, set a table at the front of the church and dress it with the white linen tablecloth. Place the cross in the middle towards the back, the chalice and paten in front of the cross, the candles to the left and right and the Bible to one side. Put the bread on the paten and some fruit juice in the chalice. Have the jug of fruit juice and the cups ready for the children.

Teaching area

The Communion table or altar rail.

▶ ▶ ▶

Aim

To discover that Holy Communion is a celebration meal for Christians. This will be a simple re-enactment to show a typical example of the service, based on the Anglican liturgy from *Common Worship*. As part of the demonstration, the storyteller may read the words in place of a member of clergy. In the worldwide church, there are many different ways of sharing this special act of worship. However, it is the custom of the church that only those who have been baptized are permitted to receive this sacrament.

Action

Gather the children around the Communion table or altar rail.

Time allocation

 15 minutes

 STORYTELLER'S SCRIPT

This table is known by a variety of different names. Sometimes it is called the Communion table, or the Lord's table. Sometimes, it is known as the altar. The table reminds Christians of a very special event, which took place near the end of Jesus' life. On the night before he died, Jesus ate a last supper with his closest friends. During the meal, he used the bread and the wine to teach his friends how to remember him after his death. He did this in a very special way. Taking the bread, he thanked God for it and said, 'This is my body, which is given for you. Eat this and remember me.' Taking the cup of wine, he lifted it up and thanked God for it. Then he said, 'This is my blood, and with it God makes his new agreement with you. Drink this and remember me' (1 Corinthians 11:24–25).

The word 'communion' reminds us that we 'come into a union' with God and with each other when we gather together to share bread and wine at this special service. Holy Communion is also known as the Eucharist, which means 'thanksgiving'. This reminds us that Jesus said 'thank you' to God for the symbols of bread and wine, but it also reminds Christians to say 'thank you' to Jesus for making it possible for people everywhere to be friends with God through Jesus' life, death and resurrection. Some Christians call the service 'the Lord's Supper', because it reminds them of the last supper that Jesus ate with his friends and also that Jesus taught that we should love one another. Finally, a very old name is the 'Mass'. This word comes from the Latin for 'dismissal' and reminds Christians of the words at the very end of the service: 'Go out to love and serve the Lord.'

At this point, invite someone to light the candles under supervision, preferably using a candle lighter, or light them yourself.

When we celebrate a birthday, we often light candles. At Holy Communion, candles are lit because it is a special party in which the whole family of the church celebrates that Jesus is 'the light for the world'.

Jesus taught us to stop arguing and fighting with each other and to live in peace with one another and with God. During the service of Holy Communion, Christians remember this by inviting everyone to end any arguments they may have with each other, and make peace. To help to show that they mean what they say, they offer each other a hand for friendship. They shake hands with everyone, saying, 'Peace be with you'.

Invite the children to shake hands with each other as a sign of being at peace, saying 'Peace be with you' as they do so. Then gather everyone in a circle around the Bible on the Communion table.

During the service of Holy Communion, the story of the last supper is read from the Bible. Jesus had some sad news and happy news to tell his friends. The sad news was that he was going to die a cruel death at the hands of the Roman soldiers. The happy news was that God would bring him back to life in a new way. So the Holy Communion celebration is both sad and happy. You can read the story of the last supper in Luke's Gospel (Luke 22:14–23).

During the service, Christians remember what they believe about Jesus by saying, 'Christ has died; Christ is risen; Christ will come again.'

The children could repeat each line of the above, if desired.

Every time Christians meet to share Holy Communion together, they believe that they are eating and drinking with Jesus in a very special way, so Jesus is with them in their hearts and minds.

At this point, the storyteller may share out the bread and the fruit juice among the children, if desired.

At the end of the service of Holy Communion, the minister closes the service by reminding the people that, now they have eaten with Jesus, they should take Jesus home with them and try to live more like him each day, by being generous, forgiving others, and showing love to everyone they meet, just as Jesus would have done. The final words of the service are 'Go in peace to love and serve the Lord', to which the people reply, 'In the name of Christ. Amen.' The word 'amen' means 'I agree'.

———◆———

Follow-up

Give each child a learning quote card and ask the children to write a sentence on the card about their learning experience during the Holy Communion re-enactment. The cards can be used later to build a folder or illustrate a school display in the classroom.

Finish by asking if there are any questions. When the group is ready, direct them to the next storytelling area.

Living worship: Music

Preparation

 You will need:

- Choir robes
- A processional cross
- Access to bell rope (if bells are available)
- A cassette or CD player
- A selection of recorded worship music
- A *Living Church* construction model
- Music storyboard card photocopied from page 62 (one per child if they are building a project folder)
- Learning quote cards photocopied from page 57 (one per child)

Teaching area

This re-enactment will use all three areas of the church: chancel, nave and tower.

Aim

To discover that the whole church building is used to make music to praise God. The chancel amplifies the choir's songs of worship. The organ is often placed in the nave, where the organist leads the congregation in hymns. Finally, the church bells ring out from the tower. This re-enactment encourages us to understand how worship involves the musical gifts of each person.

Action

Begin by gathering the children where a choir would sit. This would normally be in the chancel, but other areas are sometimes used in different church buildings.

Time allocation

 15 minutes

STORYTELLER'S SCRIPT

This is where the church choir sits. What do you think a choir does? The choir helps the whole congregation to sing hymns and songs of praise to God. The choir normally sits in the chancel. (*Explain if this is not the case in your local church.*) When we look around us, we see that the chancel is like a small church inside the church. The chancel makes the singing louder. Let's sing one note together. We will all stop together when I make this sign (*raise your hand*). Listen carefully when the singing stops. What did you notice?

Ask the group to move from the chancel and process through the nave to the choir vestry or anteroom, if there is one.

The choir not only leads the singing, but also helps to show the congregation how to worship. In many churches, a choir procession is intended to show everyone that something important is about to begin.

If the choir is agreeable, invite some of the children to try on the choir robes. How do they feel? Organize the group into a procession in pairs, perhaps in order of height.

Invite a responsible person (child or church helper) to be the 'crucifer', the person who carries the processional cross. This person leads the choir procession.

Play some processional music on the organ or on a CD and invite the group to process slowly and quietly behind the crucifer up the length of the nave towards the chancel, trying not to disturb the other groups in their activities as they do so.

How did it feel, walking in a procession? Do you think it would make other people in church pay attention?

As part of its worship, the church may use many different styles of music. Most common of all is organ music. Most churches will have a pipe organ, or a smaller electric organ. Some churches also have a piano (point out where the piano is situated if your church has one). Other churches use modern instruments, such as guitars and drums, or classical instruments, such as flutes, recorders, violins or cellos for some of their services. I wonder if any of you have ever played an instrument in a church service?

Make a procession to the organ and gather the whole group so that they can see the keyboard.

Why do you think that the organ is such a popular instrument in churches? The organ makes a rich, vibrant sound, which reflects the desire of the people to praise God in the very best way they can. The organ also produces a wide range of sounds, which makes it ideal for leading the singing, or accompanying the processions. Let's listen to some of the sounds that the organ can make.

If an organist is present, ask him or her to demonstrate a variety of the different sounds that can be created by hands and feet on the organ. Alternatively, use a recording of organ music to demonstrate the range.

Church music is used around the world to help people worship God. Let's listen to some different styles of music from around the world. Can you guess which parts of the world the different kinds of worship music come from? I wonder which piece most helps you to think about God?

Play a selection of the different styles of music available on CD. You may find examples of some of the suggestions below in your local library.

✤ The music of Taizé comes from the Taizé monastic community in France.
✤ The music of the Russian Orthodox Church has a very rich-sounding harmony.

✤ Black Gospel choir music is a mixture of the enthusiastic rhythmic style of Afro-American origin and popular, easy-to-understand lyrics.
✤ Cathedral music is often seen as the classical style of Anglican worship.
✤ Contemporary Christian music bands have created a style of modern worship that is becoming increasingly popular with today's congregations.

Process the children to the tower (or steeple) if you have one.

Can anyone tell me in what part of the church building we are standing? Our *Living Church* construction model shows us where we are. Many hundreds of years ago, towers were often added to church buildings to give the local people somewhere to hide if they were under attack. That is why the tower has strong walls and a small thick door. However, towers were also an ideal place to hang huge bells. The bells are located high above us and are used to make public announcements, such as striking the time (if the tower has a tower clock), or announcing that a service is about to begin and encouraging people to come and join in. The bell is also used to announce weddings, or tolling (ringing) the age of a person at a funeral. The bell may also be used to sound a warning in times of invasion, or to celebrate the end of a war.

If the bell rope is easily and safely accessible, invite some of the children to toll the bell with supervision. (NB: in the interests of safety, and for reasons of insurance, it is not advisable to take children up a bell tower to see the bells.)

——— ✦ ———

Follow-up

Give each child a learning quote card and ask the children to write a sentence on the card about their learning experience during the storytelling about music. The cards can be used later to build a folder or illustrate a school display in the classroom.

Finish by asking if there are any questions. When the group is ready, direct them to the next storytelling area.

Living worship: Marriage

Preparation

> **✂ You will need:**
> - ✿ Banns book
> - ✿ Rings
> - ✿ Vestments (optional)
> - ✿ Props for the 'bride' and 'groom', such as a veil and a bow-tie
> - ✿ Sheet music or CD of Wagner's *Bridal March*
> - ✿ Sheet music or CD of other hymns or songs suitable for a wedding
> - ✿ A CD player
> - ✿ Mock-up of a wedding certificate
> - ✿ Confetti (optional)
> - ✿ Wedding storyboard card photocopied from page 63 (one per child if they are building a project folder)
> - ✿ Learning quote cards photocopied from page 57 (one per child)

Prepare the children for their different roles as set out below. Invite the children taking roles to be ready with their wedding props, such as a veil for the bride and a bow-tie for the groom. Other members of the 'wedding party' may have hats or other dressing-up clothes to wear.

Divide up the remainder of the group into the bride's family and friends and bridegroom's family and friends. Invite adult helpers to help prepare children for their roles, and allocate adults to supervise the children in the different teaching areas.

Teaching area

Instruct the children to position themselves before the 'wedding service' begins, according to the role they are playing, as follows:

❖ Bride, bride's father and bridesmaids stand inside the main door, with the bride's father on the left-hand side of the bride and the bridesmaids behind her.

❖ Bridegroom and best man stand in front of the minister or storyteller at the front of the church, with the best man to the right of the bridegroom.

❖ Bell ringers, with adult helper, stand ready by the bells.

❖ Organist (or CD player) is made ready to play wedding music.

❖ Seat the rest of the children in the seats or pews at the front of the church. Traditionally, looking towards the front of the church, the family and friends of the bride sit on the left-hand side and the family and friends of the groom sit on the right-hand side.

Aim

To discover that, in church weddings, we ask God to help a couple in their marriage. This will be a simple re-enactment to show a typical example of the service, based on the Anglican liturgy. As part of the demonstration, the storyteller may read the words in place of a minister. The celebration of marriage, like baptism, is built around lifelong promises. In the wedding service, the couple promise to support each other and invite God to share in their new life together. The wedding service is one of the high points of the *Living Church* experience, with all the activity groups coming together to make this a big event in which everyone takes part.

Action

Before the re-enactment, take time to choose who will take the following roles and, once the children have been given their roles, talk them through what might be expected. Ask each to choose an imaginary first name for the person they are going to be, and surnames for their imaginary families.

- ❖ Bride
- ❖ Bride's father
- ❖ Bridesmaids
- ❖ Bridegroom
- ❖ Best man
- ❖ Families of the bride and bridegroom
- ❖ Friends of the bride and the bridegroom (the rest of the group)
- ❖ Bell ringers
- ❖ CD player operator (if no organist is available)

Time allocation

 15 minutes

 STORYTELLER'S SCRIPT

The minister or storyteller announces the wedding with the 'banns book'.

**Minister/
storyteller:** It is the law in England that, before two people can marry in church, they have to announce that they wish to marry by having their names read out in church on three successive Sundays before the ceremony can take place. This is done in order to establish that they are not already married to other people. It is called reading the 'banns of marriage'. If either partner is already married, someone who hears the banns could warn the minister not to go ahead with the wedding. If no objections are made, the wedding must then take place within three months of the final reading of the banns.

(To the congregation) I publish the banns of marriage between *(chosen name of the imaginary groom)* bachelor of this parish and *(chosen name of the imaginary bride)* spinster of the parish of *(name of a nearby church)*. If anyone knows any reason why these two people should not marry, you are to declare it now.

When everyone is ready and in their places, the minister or storyteller instructs the following people to begin playing their part in the wedding service.

- First of all, the bell ringer(s) peal the bell.
- Next, the organist plays the bridal march (or the CD player operator plays the music from a CD).
- When the music starts, the congregation stands.
- As soon as the congregation is standing, the bride and her father walk slowly down the main aisle of the church. The bridesmaids walk behind the bride and her father. The bride joins the bridegroom and best man in front of the minister or storyteller (she stands on the left-hand side of the groom). The bridesmaids stand behind the bride and the bride's father steps to the left-hand side, close to the bridal party.

**Minister/
storyteller:** Welcome to *(name of church)*. In the presence of God, Father, Son and Holy Spirit we have come together to witness the marriage of *(name of bridegroom)* and *(name of bride)*, to pray for God's blessing on them and to share in their joy as we celebrate their love.

Marriage is a gift from God, in which husband and wife grow together in love and trust and are united with one another in heart, body and mind. Marriage is a way of life made holy by God. *(Names of couple)* are now entering this way of life. They will each give their consent, make solemn vows and, in token of this, they will each give and receive a ring.

A hymn or song could be sung at this point if desired.

**Minister/
storyteller:** *(Name of groom)*, will you take *(name of bride)* to be your wife? Will you love her, comfort her, honour and protect her and, forsaking all others, be faithful to her as long as you both shall live?

At this point, the groom would reply, 'I will', but today I will say the words on his behalf.

Minister/storyteller then turns to the bride.

Minister/storyteller: *(Name of bride)*, will you take *(name of groom)* to be your husband? Will you love him, comfort him, honour and protect him and, forsaking all others, be faithful to him as long as you both shall live?

At this point, the bride would reply, 'I will', but today I will say the words on her behalf.

Minister/storyteller then turns to the bride's father.

Minister/storyteller: Who brings this woman to be married to this man?

Father: I do.

The father hands the minister/storyteller his daughter's right hand. The father takes his seat in one of the front pews. The minister/storyteller then joins the hands of the bride and groom.
   The minister/storyteller turns to the groom and speaks the words of the promise a line at a time, waiting for the groom to repeat the words of his promise.

Minister/storyteller/groom: I, *(groom's name)* take you *(bride's name)* to be my wife, for better, for worse, for richer, for poorer, in sickness and in health, to love and to cherish, till death do us part; in the presence of God I make this vow.

The minister/storyteller turns to the bride and speaks the words of the promise a line at a time, waiting for the bride to repeat the words of her promise.

Minister/storyteller/bride: I, *(bride's name)* take you *(groom's name)* to be my husband, for better, for worse, for richer, for poorer, in sickness and in health, to love and to cherish, till death do us part; in the presence of God I make this vow.

The minister/storyteller asks the best man for the rings. The best man can now sit down.

Minister/storyteller: These rings are symbols of the promises of unending love and faithfulness they have made to each other.

The minister offers the groom the ring for the bride, and the groom pretends to hold it on her finger. The minister says these words a line at a time and the groom repeats them a line at a time.

Minister/storyteller/groom: *(Name of bride)*, I give you this ring as a sign of our marriage… all that I am I give to you, and all that I have I share with you, within the love of God, Father, Son and Holy Spirit.

The minister offers the bride the ring for the groom, and the bride pretends to hold it on his finger. The minister says these words a line at a time and the bride repeats them a line at a time.

Minister/storyteller/bride: *(Name of groom)*, I give you this ring as a sign of our marriage… all that I am I give to you, and all that I have I share with you, within the love of God, Father, Son and Holy Spirit.

In the presence of God and before this congregation, *(name of groom)* and *(name of bride)* have made their marriage promises. I therefore proclaim that they are husband and wife.

Everyone sits or kneels for the prayers.

Minister/

storyteller: Lord Jesus, we ask you to bless *(name of groom)* and *(name of bride)* in their marriage. Amen.

Everyone

together: Our Father in heaven, hallowed be your name, your kingdom come, your will be done, on earth as in heaven. Give us today our daily bread. Forgive us our sins as we forgive those who sin against us. Lead us not into temptation but deliver us from evil. For the kingdom, the power, and the glory are yours now and for ever. Amen.

Minister/

storyteller: In the Church of England, the bride and groom, together with two witnesses, complete legal documents recording their marriage. They are given a copy of this document to prove they are legally married.

A pretend marriage document could be produced, which the bride, the groom, the minister/storyteller and two others (bride's and groom's mothers or fathers) sign in their pretend names.

Minister/

storyteller: May God Almighty bless you and make you strong in faith and love, defend you on every side, and guide you in truth and peace. Amen.

The bride and groom turn and walk together to the back of church, followed by the bridesmaids. Everyone else stays in his or her seat until the bride and groom have left the church. If the minister of the church has given permission, you may like to invite some of the children to throw confetti outside the church. This is a great photo opportunity, but you must seek permission from the children and parents to take photos of any of the activities. If

permission is given, photographs of the occasion can be used as part of a display as part of the Living Church project.

— ◆ —

Follow-up

Give each child a learning quote card and ask the children to write a sentence on the card about their learning experience during the storytelling about marriage. The cards can be used later to build a folder or illustrate a school display in the classroom.

Finish by asking if there are any questions. When the group is ready, direct them to the next storytelling area.

Living worship: funeral

Preparation

 You will need:

- Candles
- A cross or crucifix
- A shoebox
- A wind-up toy
- Flowers
- A plain wooden stool
- A green cloth
- Sand or earth
- Living things activity sheet photocopied from page 65 (one per child)
- Funeral storyboard card photocopied from page 64 (one per child if they are building a project folder)
- Learning quote cards photocopied from page 57 (one per child)

Teaching area

Find a place in the church where there is a tomb, family plaque in memory of someone's life, or a gravestone laid into the floor.

Aim

To discover how a Christian funeral sensitively explains that all natural life finally comes to an end, either through illness, accident, or old age when a body is simply worn out. Funerals remind us that every life is precious to God. A Christian funeral recalls the resurrection hope that Jesus Christ offered to his church at the first Easter: the wonderful news that there is life beyond death in the presence of God, free from fear and pain. Eternal life gives hope of God's wonderful, loving acceptance, joyful freedom and peace of mind, and unity with those who have gone before us. The storyteller script below is a simple re-enactment to

▶ ▶ ▶

show a typical example of the service, based on the Anglican liturgy in *Common Worship*. As part of the demonstration, the storyteller may read the words in place of a minister.

Action

To introduce the subject, gather the children near to the tomb, family plaque or gravestone and seat them in nearby pews or chairs. To re-enact the funeral service, seat the children in the pews or chairs in the nave of the church. Have ready the shoebox and the wind up-toy.

Time allocation

 15 minutes

Pastoral notes

In today's society, it is very possible that most children will not have experienced a funeral service in the same way that generations before them would have done. Alongside the services of baptism and marriage, the funeral service remains one of the main occasions when non-churchgoers have contact with a church. It is important to note that church-based funerals focus not just on the death, but on celebrating the whole life of the deceased. This session works best in small activity groups, allowing the storyteller and helpers more time to support the children. It is useful to place this session in the same rotation as the living churchyard session, which links death and the church as a sanctuary for all life.

Some children may ask questions about what we mean by the soul or spiritual dimension of a person. The illustration below may help.

The Christian understanding of what it means to be a human being comes from the Bible. The Bible teaches that every person has been uniquely created with a physical body, a conscious mind (the brain) and, connecting everything together, a spirit, or soul. Therefore, each one of us is more than a physical body of skin, bones and brain. At the heart of every single human is our spiritual being—our soul. The spiritual part of a person gives direction and meaning to the body and brain.

Explaining body and soul sensitively could be made less emotional by illustrating the soul, in loose terms, as a personal computer. The computer is more than the hardware we can see; it's the information (the software) we can't see that makes the computer what it is. If the computer's hardware is damaged or worn out, it may be the end of the old computer, but the software is not lost: it can be downloaded to a new computer. The Bible tells us that when we die, our soul (the spiritual part of us) returns to God and we are given a new heavenly body, just as the software can be downloaded from an old computer and given new life in a new computer. Human body: skin, bones, brain = computer hardware. Human spirit or soul = computer software.

When talking about death and eternal life, try not to project your own feelings or fears on to children. Children are often very matter-of-fact in their understanding of death. Many children are simply curious about death because it is a subject not normally discussed in everyday life.

NB: Many families choose cremation rather than burial for the person who has died. This ceremony takes place away from the church, at a crematorium. The part of the funeral service known as the committal refers to either burial or cremation. For the purpose of this re-enactment, we have chosen to explain the traditional churchyard burial, especially as this will link with the session about the churchyard as a sanctuary for wildlife.

STORYTELLER'S SCRIPT

A Christian funeral enables people to come together at the time of a sad occasion, when they remember the life of someone who has died. The Bible reminds us of the natural world we live in, that all living things are born, give birth to a new generation, grow older and eventually wear out and die.

Give out copies of the 'Living things' activity sheet and ask the children to guess how long each living thing would be expected to live.

Next, using a wind-up toy, demonstrate how the spring slowly unwinds until there is no more 'life' in it. This is a bit like people. Over many years, our bodies slowly run out of energy and eventually we die when everything stops working.

After the demonstration, move the children into the pews or seats in the nave of the church in

readiness for the re-enactment of the funeral service.

Storyteller: When someone dies, it is traditional in the Christian community to put the dead person's body in a special box called a coffin.

Put the wind-up toy into the shoebox.

Storyteller: Around the world, coffins come in all kinds of colours and designs: some with pictures or carvings of Jesus with his closest friends, others decorated with a cross or some flowers. If you were to decorate a coffin for someone who had died, what pictures or things would you put on the coffin to remind us of that person's life? Sometimes, a coffin is decorated with the person's favourite colour, footballers, pictures of the countryside, or beautiful flowers. All these things are marks of respect for the person who has died.

Today, we will be using this shoebox as an imaginary coffin.

Place some flowers on the shoebox and place the shoebox on the wooden stool in the main aisle at the front of the church.

Storyteller: We have come here today to remember before God our brother Fred, and to give thanks to God for his long life. We will commit his body to be buried and comfort one another in our sadness.

Fred was a well-known character in our community and well liked by us all. Fred was born 88 years ago in a very different world from the one we live in today. He lived through many changes, but he himself never changed. He was always loving and full of the joys of life. During his lifetime, Fred worked in a variety of jobs. He left school at the age of 14 to be an apprentice in a bakery, at 17 he was called up to train in the army, and when he left the army he retrained as a builder. When he was 25, he married Ethel and they had three children: Tim, Tom and Tina. When Fred retired, he took up gardening and many people in the community will miss seeing his happy face as he worked in his garden. Today we are sad, because Fred is no longer with us, but happy that we knew Fred as a friend.

At times of sadness, the Bible can give us comfort and hope from God. In this famous reading from the Bible, Jesus knows he is about to die and promises his closest friends that he will show them a new life with God after we die.

'Jesus said to his disciples, "Don't be worried! Have faith in God and have faith in me. There are many rooms in my Father's house. I wouldn't tell you this, unless it was true. I am going there to prepare a place for each of you. After I have done this, I will come back and take you with me. Then we will be together"' (John 14:1–3).

A Christian funeral helps people to share their sadness when someone dies, but Jesus says that we needn't be worried, because we also celebrate a new hope. When he miraculously came alive again on that first Easter Day, Jesus showed us that there is a new life beyond death. This is such wonderful news that his friends began to spread the good news of new life as far and wide as they could. Gradually, the Christian church began to grow, and still today continues to share the good news that Jesus has gone ahead to prepare a place for us.

Together we say goodbye to Fred and give him back to God, our maker and rescuer. Let us be silent for a moment as we say our goodbyes.

God, our creator and rescuer, in your power Jesus broke free of death. Believing in your power to give us the gift of new life, we say goodbye to Fred in the hope that you will give him eternal life in your presence. In Jesus' name we pray this prayer. Amen.

The minister or storyteller forms a procession bearing the shoebox coffin and leads the children into the churchyard, or another area of the church with tombs or memorial wall plaques. Put the shoebox on the ground between some of the gravestones and gather the group around. Invite some of the children to drop a little earth or sand on to the coffin while the following words are being read:

Storyteller: We have entrusted Fred to God's mercy, and now we commit his body to the ground. Earth to earth, ashes to ashes, dust to dust; in sure and certain hope of the resurrection to eternal life through our Lord Jesus Christ. Amen.

Cover the box with a green cloth to close the service. If desired, you could finish the session by making a simple cardboard gravestone and asking the children what they would like to put on Fred's gravestone.

———◆———

 Follow-up

Give each child a learning quote card and ask the children to write a sentence on the card about their learning experience during the funeral re-enactment. The cards can be used later to build a folder or illustrate a school display in the classroom.

Finish by asking if there are any questions. Be aware of treating sensitive issues with care and respecting the feelings and privacy of vulnerable children. If possible, link this session with the living churchyard session, which focuses on the wildlife that can be found in the fresh air of the churchyard. When the group is ready, direct them to the next storytelling area.

The living churchyard

Preparation

 You will need:

- To check that children have waterproof footwear and outdoor clothing
- Pencils
- Wildlife activity sheet photocopied from page 66 (one per child)
- Learning quote cards photocopied from page 57 (one per child)

Before the children come into the churchyard, talk with them about what a special place it is. Explain that for many local families, perhaps including their own, this is a sacred place, and we can easily upset relatives if we don't show respect. We show our respect by not running or climbing on monuments or gravestones.

Teaching area

The churchyard. Check the access around the churchyard and set the church wall or fence as the boundary. Make sure the class understand that they must stay within this boundary and not stray into the surrounding roads. For some children, the churchyard may seem like an adventure playground. However, it is most important that they do not play with the monuments, which can be unstable and may be prone to crumble or fall if rocked.

Aim

To discover that churchyards (and graveyards) are sacred places where people go to remember people they have loved. They are places where we act respectfully, and they are also enjoyable places of peacefulness. Churchyards are far from gloomy places: they are alive with flowers, insects,

▶ ▶ ▶

trees, birds and small animals. Churchyards are sanctuaries that protect our wildlife. We can discover that they have a place in 'nature's jigsaw'.

Action

Gather the children in the churchyard.

Time allocation

 15 minutes

 STORYTELLER'S SCRIPT

Welcome to *(name of church)* churchyard. If we call the church building 'the house of God', then the churchyard can be called 'God's garden'. Do you know what is so special about a churchyard? A churchyard is also known as a graveyard, because this is the place where we bury the coffin after a funeral service. For many people, this is a very special place: it is where they can come to remember a person who has died. Because it is such a special place, we must remember to be on best behaviour so that we don't upset anyone who comes to remember a person in his or her family who has died.

How do you think people find the place where their friend or relative has been buried? People mark the grave with a gravestone, giving the name and details of the person who has died. Let's look at the gravestones around us. How many different shapes of gravestones can you see? Why do you think those shapes have been chosen? Modern gravestones are often rectangular, but Victorian gravestones were carved in the shape of crosses, pillars, tombs, and even statues of angels and people. The friends and relatives were probably trying to say something about what they believed by choosing different stones.

Working in twos or threes, I wonder if we can find three things:

✤ The oldest stone with the earliest date (for example, 1713).
✤ The oldest person (for example, the dates 1810–1890 mean that the person lived to be 80 years old).
✤ Clues about a person's life (for example, their job or profession).

Remember: walk, don't run, and don't touch the gravestones. They belong to the friends and families of the people who have died. They are very special.

After a few minutes, call the children together and review the things the groups have discovered.

The second part of our activity is to discover that not only is the churchyard a special place for people to come with their memories, but it is also a sanctuary, a safe place for wildlife to live and grow. Look around you as quietly as you can. What different kinds of plant life can you see? Can you see grass, moss, clover, flowers, bushes, different kinds of trees? Look around: can you see or hear any wildlife or clues that they were here? Can you see mini-beasts like snails, ants, butterflies or ladybirds? Can you hear or see birds? Can you see nests, or a rabbit or hedgehog?

Churchyards have been protected for hundreds of years to prevent people from building or disturbing anything, so they are perfect homes for wildlife—plants, birds and animals. This is another reason to be careful when we explore a churchyard, because it is the home of lots of living creatures and plants, some of which live here because it is a safe place to be.

To help us explore, we have a wildlife activity sheet. Some of the plants, like the trees, are very big; some insects are very small; some birds are friendly and some animals are very shy, but they all live in this place. Welcome to their home. Look at the activity sheet and, working in twos or threes,

tick any of the things you can see, such as birds, leaves or flowers. How many living things can you find in this wildlife sanctuary? Remember, look, but don't touch the creatures or plants. This is their home and we are visitors. Churchyards are a 'sanctuary', a safe place, for wildlife, where they are protected.

After a few minutes, recall the children and review the variety of plants, birds and creatures the groups have discovered.

We are part of nature's jigsaw. Look carefully at your 'Living things' activity sheet. You will see that each living thing is joined to the next as if it were a jigsaw piece. Nature is just like a living jigsaw. Just like jigsaw pieces, all the different plants, insects, birds and animals are important. Like pieces in a jigsaw, they all fit together, so every living thing has a place and needs other living things for everything to be complete. Even the things that we think are horrible have their place; they would leave a gap in the jigsaw if they died out. Can you see how some birds need plants, and plants need insects, and how it all fits together? People are just one part of the jigsaw. We have a responsibility to keep this special place safe.

———— ✦ ————

Follow-up

Give each child a learning quote card and ask the children to write a sentence on the card about their learning experience during the storytelling about the living churchyard. The cards can be used later to build a folder or illustrate a school display in the classroom.

Finish by asking if there are any questions. When the group is ready, direct them to the next storytelling area.

Living worship: Vestments

Preparation

 You will need:

- ✪ A selection of the vestments used by the clergy in the church
- ✪ Church vestments activity sheet photocopied from pages 67–68 on to medium-weight white card (one sheet per child)
- ✪ Colouring materials
- ✪ Scissors
- ✪ Learning quote cards photocopied from page 57 (one per child)

Arrange for the minister of the church to display the vestments kept in church for people leading services. Churches vary in their choice of vestments. Some ministers choose to wear a cassock, surplice and scarf; some a cassock alb and stole; some a simple clerical shirt and collar. Some choose not to wear any special religious clothing at all. The session describes the full range of vestments available, but you will need to discuss with the minister what is the normal practice for the church you are visiting.

Teaching area

A vestry or suitable area of the church where the vestments can be displayed.

Aim

To discover why some, but not all, churches have special clothing known as vestments for the people who lead worship. Vestments are symbols of spiritual significance. They are signs of church authority and public service, as well as celebrating the different seasons of the Christian year through colour and design.

▶ ▶ ▶

Action

Gather the children in the designated area, but do not let them touch any of the items on display.

Time allocation

 15 minutes

 STORYTELLER'S SCRIPT

There is a wonderful range of traditions in the worldwide Christian church when it comes to wearing special clothes for leading worship. Some church leaders wear everyday clothes on purpose to help the congregation feel more relaxed. Some churches expect their clergy and choir to put on special religious clothing. The special clothes that clergy and choirs wear are known as vestments. The style of religious clothing has been handed down through history.

Can you think of other people who wear special clothes for their work? Can you think of a reason why people wear special clothing? Religious clothing is designed to act like a signpost: it points people towards God. Let's find out why this is.

First of all, it makes us look.

- ✤ Football teams wear team strips. In a similar way, religious clothing helps people to recognize the person who is going to lead the service.
- ✤ What do the different colours of a traffic light mean? In a similar way, vestments give different messages through the colours they display.
- ✤ When would we put on our best or special clothes? In a similar way, vestments celebrate that something special is about to happen.

Secondly, vestments make us listen.

❖ Who wears a crown when they make a speech? Just as kings or queens wear crowns, a minister wears vestments when he or she has something important to say.
❖ How can we see that someone is a police officer with authority? In the same way, vestments remind people to listen to the minister because he or she has been given authority to speak the word of God.
❖ What part of a soldier's uniform shows us who their leader is? Just as the cap badge shows us who is the leader of an army, so vestments, with their Christian symbols, remind people that Jesus is their leader.

Finally, vestments help us to learn.

❖ Before television was invented, the town crier wore special clothes to show that he or she had authority to give out news. The minister wears vestments to show people that he or she has the training and authority to speak out the good news about Jesus.
❖ In the army, soldiers wear special clothes to keep them from being seen. Vestments act like camouflage clothing. They can help people to forget about the minister as the person they know and focus on the message about Jesus Christ.

So you can see that vestments are like a spiritual uniform. They speak about God.

Invite the minister to explain the everyday religious clothes they wear. For most ministers, this is usually a clerical shirt and collar, commonly known as a 'dog collar', which no one else in the community wears. Next, invite the minister to show the basic vestments for leading worship. This may be a black cassock, or a white cassock alb. Cassocks are very much like overcoats in that they are worn on top of normal clothes. A chasuble of a seasonal colour may be worn and, for outdoor services such as burials, a thick cape may be worn.

Then show the next layer, which goes over the cassock. This may be a white surplice on top of a black cassock and a black reading scarf. Notice the simple but striking use of black and white in this type of religious uniform, which is often worn for morning and evening prayer. If available, show the children a variety of different coloured stoles used for special services, such as Holy Communion, baptisms, weddings or funerals.

Do you have a school badge on your uniform? Christian symbols on vestments have different meanings.

❖ White is used for the seasons of Christmas and Easter, and also for baptisms and weddings.
❖ Purple is used for the seasons of Advent and Lent, and also for funerals.
❖ Green is used for the seasons of Epiphany and Trinity.
❖ Red is used for the season of Pentecost and the festivals of saints.

For a more creative explanation of the colours, see the notes accompanying the session on the Christian year (p. 47). If possible, invite children to wear some of the vestments. Ask them how these special clothes make them feel. Can they remember what the different colours mean? What do the colours remind them of?

— ◆ —

 Follow-up

Give each child a copy of the church vestments activity sheet. Invite the children to colour the vestments and figure, then cut them out and dress the minister for different services, such as using a white stole for a wedding.

Alternatively, ask the children to design symbols to put on the stole for a special service, such as a baptism, a wedding, a funeral or a service of Holy Communion. Encourage them to think about the colour, shape and pattern of their design.

Finally, give each child a learning quote card and ask the children to write a sentence on the card about their learning experience during the storytelling about vestments. The cards can be used later to build a folder or illustrate a school display in the classroom.

Finish by asking if there are any questions. When the group is ready, direct them to the next storytelling area.

11

Living worship: the worldwide Church

Preparation

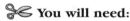 **You will need:**

- ✪ Scissors and glue
- ✪ Drawing and colouring implements
- ✪ A completed *Living Church* construction model
- ✪ Worldwide Church activity sheet photocopied from page 69 (one per child)
- ✪ Church shape activity sheet photocopied to A3 from page 70 (one per child)
- ✪ Church design furnishings sheet photocopied from page 71 (one per child)
- ✪ Church design questions sheet photocopied from page 72 (one per child)
- ✪ Learning quote cards photocopied from page 57 (one per child)

Teaching area

The whole church building.

Aim

To discover the range of designs used for church building in the worldwide Church and to show how the architecture of a building, together with the furniture, shapes the worship.

Action

You may wish to move around the church to demonstrate some of the building features.

Time allocation

 15 minutes

 STORYTELLER'S SCRIPT

Invite the children to complete the 'Worldwide Church' activity sheet by drawing a line from each church building to the map. Younger children may need help with this activity. Review the answers and talk about the many different shapes and designs. Ask the children to put a tick next to the buildings they like best. Finally, show the children the Living Church construction model.

We can see from the activity sheet that church buildings in other parts of the world are very different from a typical English church. However, although they look different from the outside, inside most of them have many things in common, such as a table for Holy Communion, a pulpit and a place for baptism.

In this session, we are going to try designing our own church building, using different styles and traditions from the worldwide Church as our guide.

In school, we sometimes arrange our seating differently depending on the occasion. For example, we may sit in a circle, or in straight lines, or in the shape of a horseshoe. Churches also choose different ways to arrange the seating. Let's try sitting in different shapes to find out which shapes we prefer and why.

Give each child a copy of each of the three remaining activity sheets.

The 'church shape' activity sheet gives a bird's-eye view of three typical shapes of church design: a cross, a rectangle and a circle. Choose the shape you like best by joining up the dots of the outside walls with a pencil.

On the 'church design questions' sheet, circle the name of the shape you have chosen and write a sentence about why you have chosen this shape of church.

Now look at the different styles of church furniture, commonly found in most churches. Church furniture has a practical function: for example, the baptistry needs to hold water, but the different designs also express different spiritual meanings. For example, some baptistries are like pools because of the spiritual importance for people to be fully immersed in the water when they are baptized. Let's think about the practical function of the furnishings in this church, and then try to guess what the spiritual meaning might be. The questions we need to ask ourselves are, 'What practical function has this in worship?' and 'What does it say about God?'

The 'church design furnishings' sheet gives you three choices for six important items that you need to include in your own church design. Choose one of the three designs for each item. On the 'church design questions' sheet, circle the number of the design you have chosen and write a few words about why you have chosen that design rather than the others. Is there a practical reason, or does it say

something about God? Once you have designed your six items, cut them out and arrange them in the shape you have chosen for your church. Take time to think about your design before you finally glue each item in place. Finally, cut out the outside shape you have chosen for your church. You may have chosen an old European-design Communion table with an up-to-date music band and a place for prayer from the traditional Russian. You have created a worldwide church!

Review the children's work and show the designs to each other.

———✦———

Follow-up

Invite the children to look around the church to find specific Christian symbols. How many can they find? What do the different symbols mean?

Next, give each child a learning quote card and ask the children to write a sentence on the card about their learning experience during the storytelling about the worldwide Church. The cards can be used later to build a folder or illustrate a school display in the classroom.

Finish by asking if there are any questions. When the group is ready, direct them to the next storytelling area.

12

The Living Church: world mission

Preparation

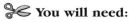 **You will need:**

- Scissors
- Glue
- Caring and sharing activity sheet photocopied from page 73 (one per child)
- Learning quote cards photocopied from page 57 (one per child)

Teaching area

Either a stained-glass window or memorial plaque to someone who showed generosity to those in need, or who preached the good news of Jesus; or a missionary information display stand.

Aim

To discover what the church community does when it is not inside the church building.

Action

Gather the children around the chosen area.

Time allocation

 15 minutes

STORYTELLER'S SCRIPT

Many people think that church is like a club for people who meet on Sundays to think about God. But when Jesus began the church, he gave his followers clear instructions that the purpose of the church was to take the good news about Jesus to everyone in the world. The Bible tells us that Jesus said, 'Go to the people of all nations and make them my disciples' (Matthew 28:19). The reason that there are Christian churches all around the world is because people did just as Jesus asked. In church, everyone is welcome: men and women, boys and girls. It doesn't matter what age, colour or race you are, or whether or not you have made mistakes in your life.

Today we have seen that there are many things in church that are very old. But the church is not a museum. We have seen that it is a living community of people who worship God together. But it is also a community that cares. The church is like God's ambulance station, where Christians come to practise their lifesaving skills of caring, forgiveness and generosity. They then go out into the world to use their skills to help people throughout the world who are suffering, sad or in great need.

Being a Christian is about two things. First of all, it is about thinking good and kind thoughts, but it doesn't stop there. The Bible tells us that Christianity is also about putting the love and forgiveness of Jesus into practical action. A man called James, who was probably Jesus' brother, wrote, 'My friends, what good is it to say you have faith, when you don't do anything to show that you really do have faith? … Faith that doesn't lead us to do good deeds is all alone and dead!'(James 2:14, 17).

Once we begin to investigate the Christian church, we realize that church is about training people on Sundays to serve others for the other six days of the week. It is about followers of Jesus putting their faith into action and helping those in need.

Give out the 'Caring and sharing' activity sheets.

The activity sheet shows all kinds of practical ways in which Christians have worked hard at putting their faith into practical action. By caring and sharing what time, love and money they have, Christians give hope to people who find themselves in very sad situations. On the sheet we can see some of the ways in which the church cares for people all around the world.

Read through the different projects on the sheet with the children and then ask them to draw a line between the words and the church activity.

———— ✦ ————

Follow-up

Give each child a learning quote card and ask the children to write a sentence on the card about their learning experience during the storytelling about world mission. The cards can be used later to build a folder or illustrate a school display in the classroom.

Finish by asking if there are any questions. When the group is ready, direct them to the next storytelling area.

13

The Christian calendar

Preparation

 You will need:

- Scissors
- Glue
- The Christian year activity sheet photocopied from page 74 (one per child)
- The Christian year resource sheet photocopied from page 75 (one per child)
- The Christian year reference sheet photocopied from page 76 (one copy only)
- Learning quote cards photocopied from page 57 (one per child)

Teaching area

The chancel, if the tradition of the church is to use coloured altar frontal cloths to mark the seasons of the year.

Aim

To explore a year in the life of a church and discover the seasonal colours and festivals that mark the progression of the Christian story through the year.

Action

Gather the children in the chancel, but make sure they have space around them and can see the altar frontal cloth.

Time allocation

 15 minutes

STORYTELLER'S SCRIPT

Just as the natural seasons of spring, summer, autumn and winter follow each other every year, so the church community keeps a pattern of spiritual seasons to mark the progress of the year. Do you have a favourite season of the year? Do you look forward to it? Why? Christians look forward to the different spiritual seasons and festivals because they are special times to celebrate important events in the Christian year, such as Christmas and Easter.

Give out the 'Christian year' activity sheets. Invite the children to study the calendar.

Notice how the calendar is shaped like a clock face. It should be read in a clockwise direction. In the four corners we see the four seasons of the year, and this gives us a clue to which festivals we will find near those seasons.

Give out the 'Christian year' resource sheets. Invite the children to cut out the pictures of the four seasons and glue each picture in its correct place. (NB: If needed, use the 'Christian year' reference sheet as a guide.)

The 360 degrees of the circle represent the 365 days of the year, so each degree represents (approximately) one day of the year. As you can see, the calendar is divided into segments like slices of pie. Look at the inner circle. Here you will see the names of the different seasons and the month in which they fall. The twelve o'clock position is the start of the year, which, for the church, is in the month of November. The first season is Advent, followed by Christmas and then

Epiphany, Lent and Easter. You will see that Christmas falls in the winter and Easter (at the five o'clock position) falls in the spring.

In nature, flowers, trees and fruit are constantly changing and growing. Their colours remind us of the seasons of the year. For example, in spring nature produces lots of green and yellow, and in autumn we see lots of brown, gold and red. The church mirrors a similar pattern of changing colours as the Christian story moves through the year. In some churches, you will see that the minister's clothing, the cloth on the Communion table and other banners or drapes change to show the seasonal colour. This reflects the changes that happen in nature and reminds people that a new season has begun and it is time to move to the next part of the Christian story. Each colour reminds people about the story that goes with the season.

❖ The season of Advent is purple. Purple is a sad colour: it reminds people of bruises and things that hurt.
❖ The season of Christmas is white. White is a pure colour: it reminds people of things that are unspoilt and clean.
❖ The season of Epiphany is green. Green is a growing colour: it reminds people of natural growing things.
❖ The season of Lent is purple. Purple is a sad colour: it reminds people of sorrow and the sad things in the world.
❖ Holy Week marks the end of the season of Lent. The colour for Holy Week is red: it reminds people of God's love and Jesus' blood as he died on the cross.
❖ The season of Easter is white. White is a pure colour: it reminds people of brand new things like a new, clean page.
❖ The season of Pentecost is red. Red is a warm colour: it reminds people of the warmth of a fire.
❖ The season of Trinity is green. Green is a growing colour; it reminds people of natural, healthy growing things.

Invite the group to colour the inner circle of their calendars according to the seasonal colour.

The outer circle of the calendar shows how the church tells the story of Jesus' life every year.

Invite the children to cut out the pictures that tell the story of Jesus' life and glue each picture in its correct place. (NB: If needed, use the 'Christian year' reference sheet as a guide.)

Let's look at what the Bible teaches in each season of the Christian year.

Advent: Advent begins on the last Sunday in November and ends on Christmas Eve. This four-week period is the time for people to prepare for Christmas. It's a time to think about what is wrong with the world, to read the Bible and pray.

Christmas: At Christmas, Christians thank God for bringing Jesus into the world as a tiny baby: the Son of God, who came to open the way to heaven.

Epiphany: Epiphany recalls the story of the three wise men who travelled to Bethlehem to worship baby Jesus, God's new king. Their story reminds people that Christianity is a worldwide family where everyone is welcomed in.

Lent: Lent starts on Ash Wednesday, six weeks before Easter. It is a time to reflect on the world's problems, to read the Bible, take time to pray and try to live in the way Jesus showed us.

Holy Week: Holy Week tells the story of the last week of Jesus' life, from the day he rode into the city of Jerusalem on a donkey (Palm Sunday) to the day he was put to death on a cross (Good Friday). It reminds people of how Jesus suffers with us and for us.

Easter: Easter is the highest point of the church's year. It is a happy time when people celebrate how Jesus proved he was the Son of God by coming alive in a new way after death (the resurrection).

Ascension: After the resurrection, there was a 40-day period when Jesus appeared to his friends and promised the coming of God's Holy Spirit as a helper and a guide. After this period, Jesus returned to his Father in heaven.

Pentecost: The Bible tells us that, after he rose to new life, Jesus promised to send God's Spirit to guide everyone who asks God for help. Pentecost celebrates the day that the Holy Spirit came. Christians believe that God's Holy Spirit still guides his church today.

Trinity: Trinity is the longest season of the church's year. It reminds people that God can be known in three important ways: first of all, as creator and owner of the world; secondly, in the person of Jesus; and, finally, in the person of God's Holy Spirit.

All Saints: In the early days of the church, many Christians were persecuted, imprisoned and even killed because of their faith. Their lives were given special recognition and they were considered to be saints. Their stories became inspirational to other Christians, helping people to be brave and not give up. Many churches have a saint as their patron and name their church after that person as an inspiration to others.

Let's look for clues about saints in this church. We can check the name of the church on the board outside, look at the stained-glass windows, or look for a painting or statue in a place of prayer. What can you find out about the saint's life? How could their life encourage Christians today to follow Jesus even when they face opposition?

Each saint has a special day when they are remembered. In some parts of the world, if you are born on a saint's day you may have their name as a second name added to your own.

— ✦ —

Follow-up

Give each child a learning quote card and ask the children to write a sentence on the card about their learning experience during the storytelling about the Christian year. The cards can be used later to build a folder or illustrate a school display in the classroom.

Finish by asking if there are any questions. When the group is ready, direct them to the next storytelling area.

The Living Church
supplementary material

The Living Church classroom display

The *Living Church* experience can leave a memorable impression on the children who participate. Producing an exhibition of the activities can be a simple but effective teaching tool. Below are some ideas for making a simple, colourful display for the classroom or school hall with the minimum amount of effort.

A BRIEF HISTORY OF CHURCH BUILDINGS

The following items can be used to set the scene for the project:

❖ The *Living Church* timeline (for greater effect, this could be enlarged and coloured in or photocopied on to coloured paper)
❖ The *Living Church* construction models (made by the children)

LIVING WORSHIP

A display can be made of the following items:

❖ Storyboards for each re-enactment (coloured in by the children)
❖ Photographs of the activities (with parental permission)
❖ Photographs of the church building, including interesting features and furnishings
❖ A selection of the learning quote cards for each session (completed by the children)
❖ A selection of the activity sheets (completed by the children)
❖ Artefacts used for the re-enactments
❖ The *Living Church* poster (coloured in by the children)
❖ Cut-out figures showing the range of vestments used by clergy

FRONT COVER FOR A LIVING CHURCH PROJECT FILE

Ask each child to create their own design for the front cover of their project folders. Information needed for the front cover may include:

❖ *Living Church* logo (designed by the child)
❖ The title *Living Church*
❖ A subtitle, such as, 'My visit to *(name of church)*'
❖ Pupil's name
❖ Pupil's year group or class name
❖ Name of school
❖ Date

The Living Church timeline

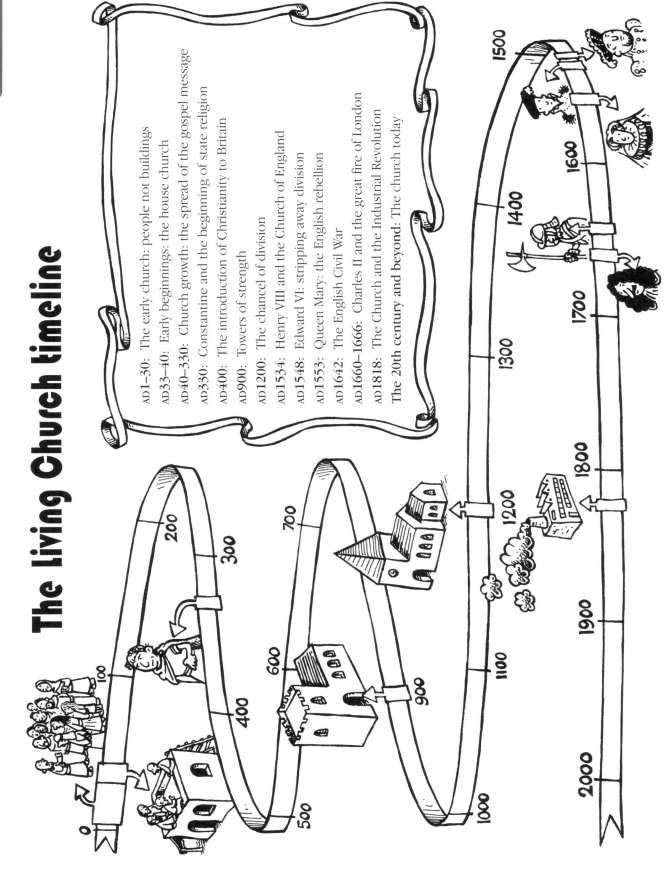

AD1–30: The early church: people not buildings

AD33–40: Early beginnings: the house church

AD40–330: Church growth: the spread of the gospel message

AD330: Constantine and the beginning of state religion

AD400: The introduction of Christianity to Britain

AD900: Towers of strength

AD1200: The chancel of division

AD1534: Henry VIII and the Church of England

AD1548: Edward VI: stripping away division

AD1553: Queen Mary: the English rebellion

AD1642: The English Civil War

AD1660–1666: Charles II and the great fire of London

AD1818: The Church and the Industrial Revolution

The 20th century and beyond: The church today

www.barnabasinschools.org.uk

Reproduced with permission from *Living in Church* published by BRF 2006 (1 84101 399 4)

The Living Church construction model

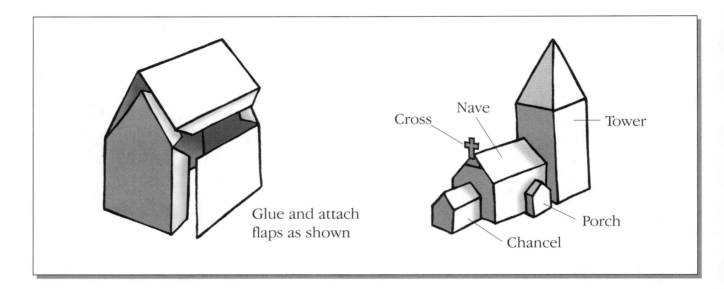

Glue and attach flaps as shown

Cross   Nave   Tower   Porch   Chancel

Chancel

Porch

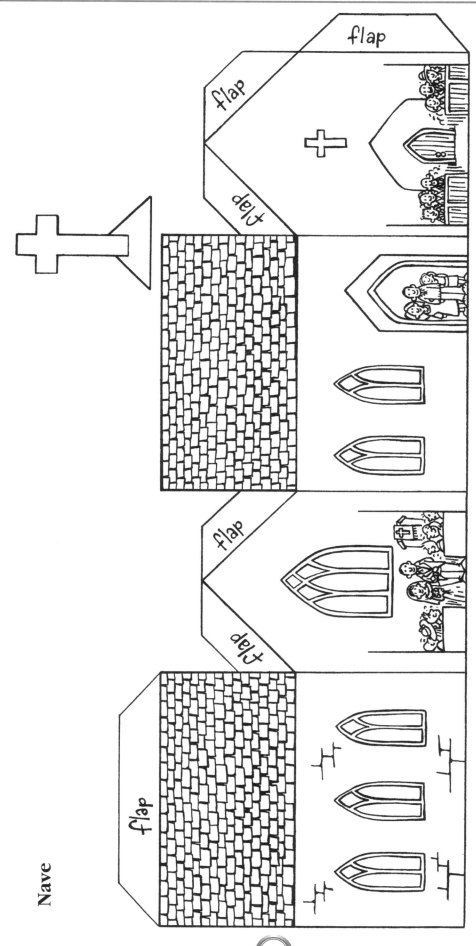

Nave

www.barnabasinschools.org.uk

Reproduced with permission from *Living in Church* published by BRF 2006 (1 84101 399 4)

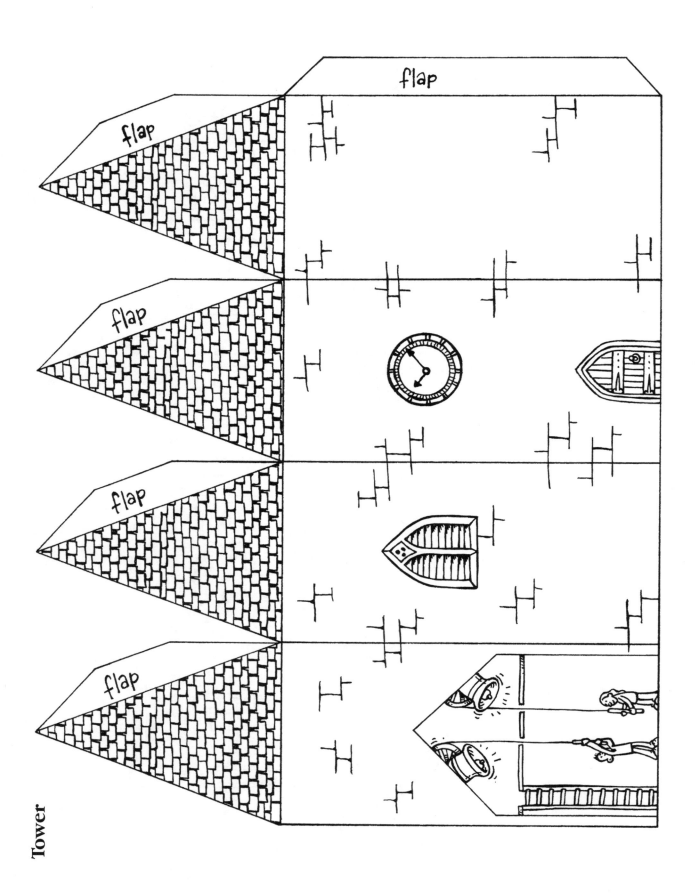

Tower

A brief history of the Living Church information sheet

1. The early church: people not buildings

Soon after the death and resurrection of Jesus, his followers became known as Christians. They met together to pray and to worship God. The word 'church' comes from the Greek adjective *kyriakos*, which means 'belonging to the Lord'. The first church was not an inanimate building, but living people, worshipping God together.

2. Early beginnings: the house church

The religious leaders of the day felt threatened by the followers of Jesus. The first Christians were hunted down and put to death or thrown into prison. For this reason, they had to meet in secret. They had no special buildings, so they met in each other's homes. Their worship included prayers, singing, sharing bread and wine together and learning to follow Jesus' teaching in the best way they could.

3. Constantine and the beginning of state religion

When Christianity became a recognized religion, people no longer had to meet in secret to worship God. Special buildings were built for public worship, village meetings and celebrations. Everyone was always welcome in this part of the church: they even held markets in the nave.

4. Towers of strength

From around the tenth century, towers were added to the west end of the nave. The church tower provided a place of safety: villagers could hide in it in times of trouble. Bells were hung in the tower to warn people if the village was under attack, and to ring out in celebration at a wedding. Most of all, the bells were used to mark the time of day and to call people to the church building where they worshipped together.

5. The chancel of division

During the 13th century, a chancel was built on the east end of the nave to separate the noise and busyness of the public area from the quietness of daily worship. This new area of the building became known as the sanctuary. It was a place for private prayer, singing, sharing bread and wine and celebrating special services, led by priests or monks.

www.barnabasinschools.org.uk
Reproduced with permission from *Living in Church* published by BRF 2006 (1 84101 399 4)

The Living Church poster

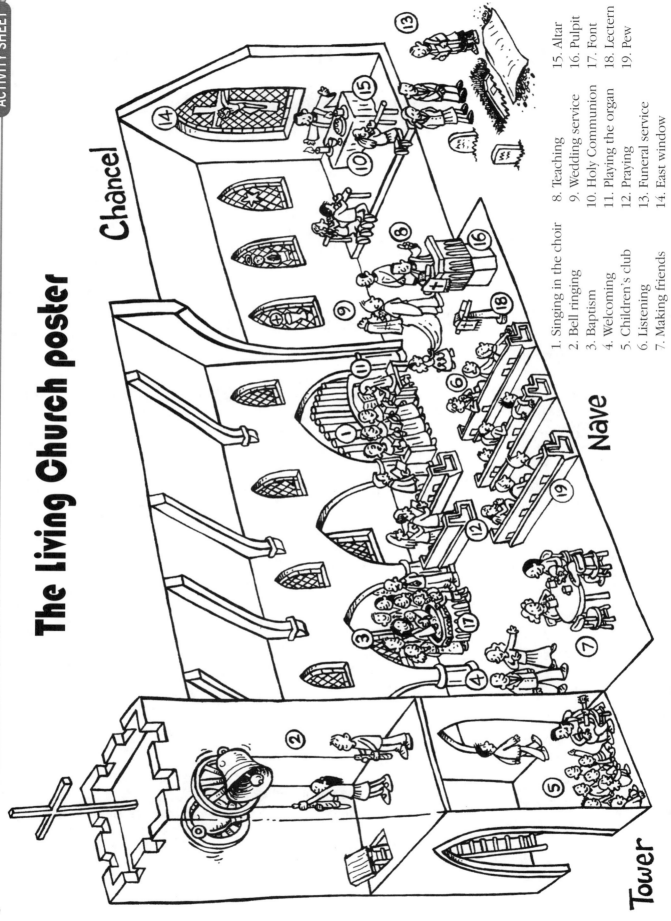

Chancel

Nave

Tower

1. Singing in the choir
2. Bell ringing
3. Baptism
4. Welcoming
5. Children's club
6. Listening
7. Making friends

8. Teaching
9. Wedding service
10. Holy Communion
11. Playing the organ
12. Praying
13. Funeral service
14. East window

15. Altar
16. Pulpit
17. Font
18. Lectern
19. Pew

Learning quote cards

Name: _____

Class: _____

Activity: (circle the topic)

Baptism

The Bible

Prayer

Holy Communion

Music

Marriage

Funeral

The living churchyard

Vestments

The worldwide Church

World mission

The Christian calendar

What I remember most about this topic is:

Name: _____

Class: _____

Activity: (circle the topic)

Baptism

The Bible

Prayer

Holy Communion

Music

Marriage

Funeral

The living churchyard

Vestments

The worldwide Church

World mission

The Christian calendar

What I remember most about this topic is:

---

www.barnabasinschools.org.uk

Reproduced with permission from *Living in Church* published by BRF 2006 (1 84101 399 4)

Baptism storyboard card

Thanking God for life

The baptismal font

Promises made by parents and godparents

The sign of the cross

The sign of the water

The sign of light

The Bible storyboard card

God loved the people of this world so much that he gave his only Son, so that everyone who has faith in him will have eternal life and never really die (John 3:16).

A famous verse from the Bible

This is the good news about Jesus Christ

An illuminated letter

The lectern

The pulpit

The pews

www.barnabasinschools.org.uk

Reproduced with permission from *Living in Church* published by BRF 2006 (1 84101 399 4)

Prayer storyboard card

Talking and listening

Praise: to say how great we think God is
Repent: to say sorry to God
Ask: to ask God for help
Yourself: to pray for things in our own lives

Kneeling or sitting to pray

Jesus said, 'I am the light for the world!' (John 8:12)

The Lord's Prayer in modern English

Our Father in heaven, hallowed be your name,
your kingdom come, your will be done
on earth as in heaven.
Give us today our daily bread.
Forgive us our sins as we forgive those
who sin against us.
Lead us not into temptation but deliver us from evil.
For the kingdom, the power and the glory are yours
now and for ever. Amen.

The Lord's Prayer in old English

Our Father who art in heaven, hallowed be thy name,
thy kingdom come, thy will be done,
on earth as it is in heaven.
Give us this day our daily bread.
Forgive us our trespasses
as we forgive those who trespass against us.
And lead us not into temptation
but deliver us from evil.
For thine is the kingdom, the power and the glory
forever and ever. Amen.

Prayer candles

Reproduced with permission from *Living in Church* published by BRF 2006 (1 84101 399 4)

Holy Communion storyboard card

The Communion table

Candles

Sharing the peace

Reading the story
of the last supper

Bread and wine

Go in peace to love and
serve the Lord

Music storyboard card

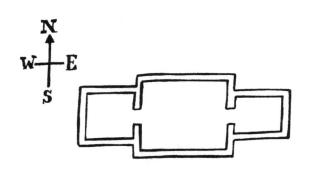

The church building

The choir

The crucifer leads a choir procession

The organ

The bells ring in the church tower

Ringing the bells

Wedding storyboard card

Making promises

Rings as a sign of
promises made

Proclaiming the marriage

Signing the register

The wedding procession

The wedding photographs

funeral storyboard card

Processing with the coffin

Welcoming the people

Giving a tribute to the person who has died

Reading from the Bible

Praying for the person who has died, and family and friends

The grave and gravestone

Living things activity sheet

Fill in the life expectancy of each of these living things.

Goldfish: _____

Elephant: _____

Human being: _____

Golden retriever: _____

Butterfly: _____

Daffodil: _____

Hamster: _____

Oak tree: _____

| 2–4 months | 300–400 years | 5–10 years | 70–80 years |
| 50–70 years | 10–12 years | 2–4 weeks | 1–2 years |

www.barnabasinschools.org.uk

Reproduced with permission from *Living in Church* published by BRF 2006 (1 84101 399 4)

Wildlife activity sheet

Vestments activity sheet

Colour in and cut out the figure and clothing and dress the minister.

Cassock Alb
White

Minister

Clerical shirt
Any colour

www.barnabasinschools.org.uk

Reproduced with permission from *Living in Church* published by BRF 2006 (1 84101 399 4)

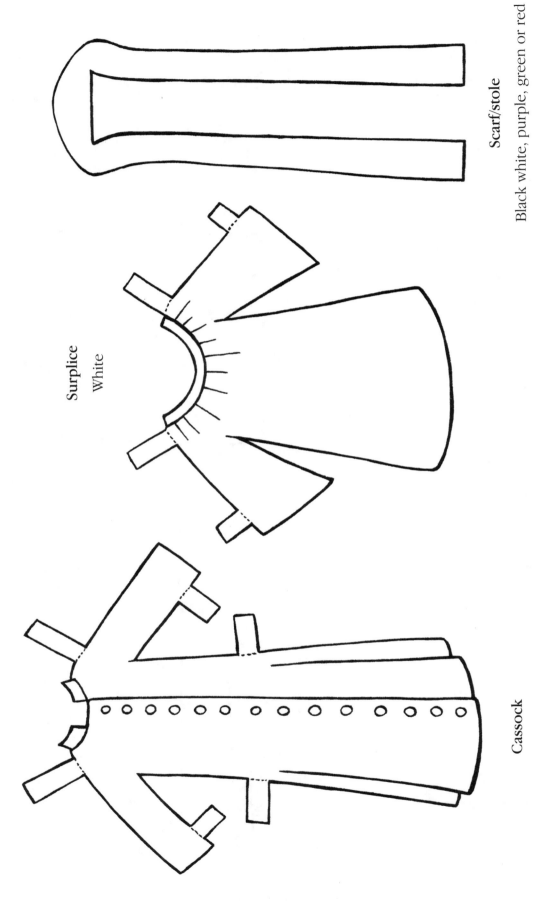

Scarf/stole

Black white, purple, green or red

Surplice

White

Cassock

Black or blue

Worldwide Church activity sheet

Draw a line from the churches to where they are on the world map.

Italian country

Mexican city

Canadian town

American country

Nigerian country

English city

Russian city

Turkish city

Korean country

American city

www.barnabasinschools.org.uk

Reproduced with permission from *Living in Church* published by BRF 2006 (1 84101 399 4)

Church shape activity sheet

Choose the floor shape for your church from the bird's-eye view of the church marked in dotted lines. Make the outside walls of your church by joining the dots to form the church building in the shape of a cross, a rectangle or a circle.

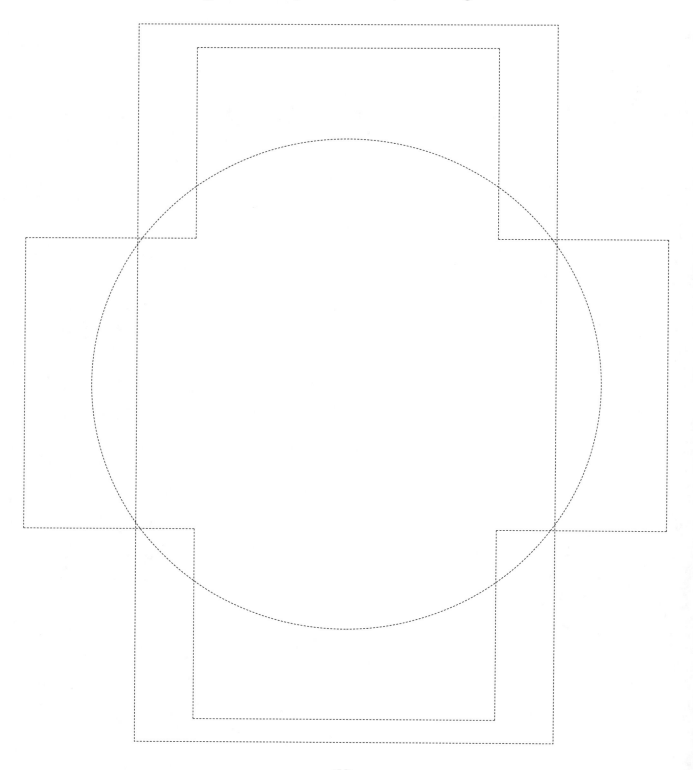

Reproduced with permission from *Living in Church* published by BRF 2006 (1 84101 399 4)

Church design furnishings sheet

	Design 1	Design 2	Design 3
Font/ Baptistry			
Places for prayer			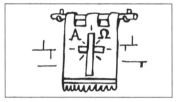
Communion table			
Pulpit/lectern			
Seating			
Musical instruments			

www.barnabasinschools.org.uk
Reproduced with permission from *Living in Church* published by BRF 2006 (1 84101 399 4)

Church design question sheet

I chose a cross/rectangle/circle shape because… _____

_____

The font/baptistry

Practically, the font or baptistry holds the water with which people are baptized. Spiritually, the water reminds us that, when we join his family, God washes away the things we have done wrong.

I chose design 1/2/3 because… _____

_____

Places for prayer

Practically, places for prayer include crosses, paintings and icons or candles. Spiritually, places for prayer are designed to help people to use their imagination when they pray to God.

I chose design 1/2/3 because… _____

_____

The Communion table

Practically, the table holds the things needed for a service of Holy Communion, such as bread, wine, a cup and plate, candles and a Bible. Spiritually, the table reminds people of the last supper Jesus ate with his closest friends on the night before he died.

I chose design 1/2/3 because… _____

_____

The pulpit/lectern

Practically, the pulpit or lectern is where the minister can place a Bible and teaching notes, and be seen by the people. Spiritually, the pulpit or lectern reminds people that the Bible has an important place in the church building.

I chose design 1/2/3 because… _____

_____

Seating

Practically, seating was introduced so that people wouldn't have to stand for the whole of the church service, although, even today, in some churches people stand and move around freely. Spiritually, the way we sit, stand or kneel affects the way we feel when we worship God.

I chose design 1/2/3 because… _____

_____

Musical instruments

Practically, musical instruments are used to help lead the worship. Spiritually, the music can help people to worship God more effectively.

I chose design 1/2/3 because… _____

_____

Caring and sharing activity sheet

Read about all the things that the church is involved in within the community, then draw a line between the words (such as 'schools') and the correct church activity.

The church is involved in campaigning for farmers in poor countries to get a fair price for their goods.

The church provides trained medical staff and ministers to help those who are dying of long-term illnesses, and gives support to their families.

The church has set up schools to provide children with a good education. These schools are often named after their church.

The church has set up hostels and gives food and clothing to care for people who have nowhere to live.

This organization was started by a vicar to help people talk when they have no one else they can talk to.

The church shares its faith with people who would not otherwise hear the good news about Jesus.

Hospitals

Hostels

Care homes

Schools

Government

Orphanages

Samaritans

Mission

Worldwide aid

Fair Trade

Hospices

The church has set up homes to care for older people who have no one else to care for them.

The church has set up homes for children with no parents, and continues to care for children today.

The church has set up hospitals to help those who are unwell, and provides chaplains to care for people.

The church shares what it has with people in many parts of the world who find themselves in long-term poverty, and gives helps in times of famine and war.

Church leaders talk to the government about difficult issues, such as poverty and employment, and gives advice about the care of families and children.

www.barnabasinschools.org.uk
Reproduced with permission from *Living in Church* published by BRF 2006 (1 84101 399 4)

The Christian year activity sheet

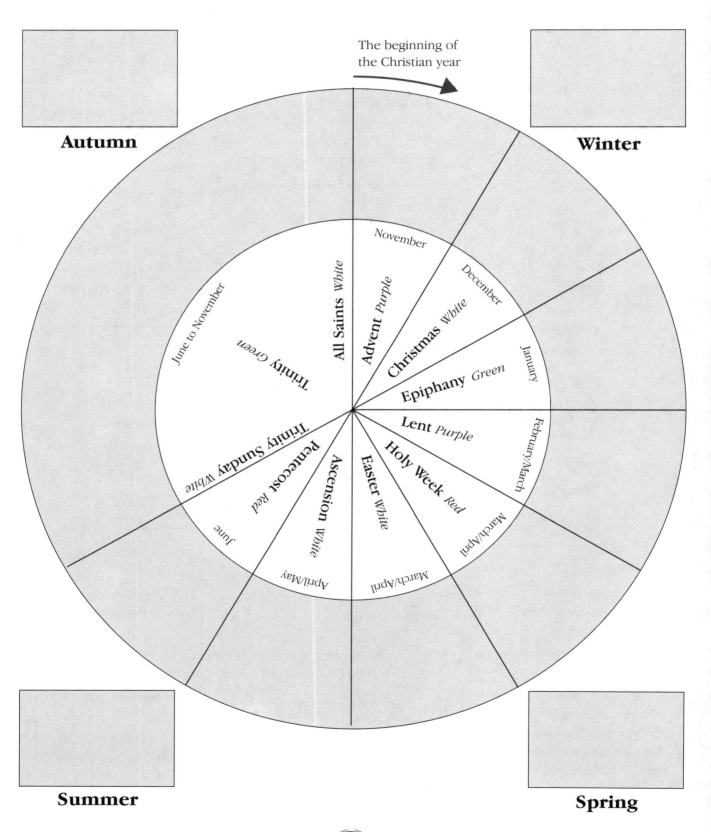

The beginning of the Christian year

Autumn

Winter

Summer

Spring

November

December

January

February/March

March/April

March/April

April/May

June

June to November

All Saints *White*

Advent *Purple*

Christmas *White*

Epiphany *Green*

Lent *Purple*

Holy Week *Red*

Easter *White*

Ascension *White*

Pentecost *Red*

Trinity Sunday *White*

Trinity *Green*

Reproduced with permission from *Living in Church* published by BRF 2006 (1 84101 399 4)

The Christian year resource sheet

Cut out the pictures and stick them in the correct places on the calendar.

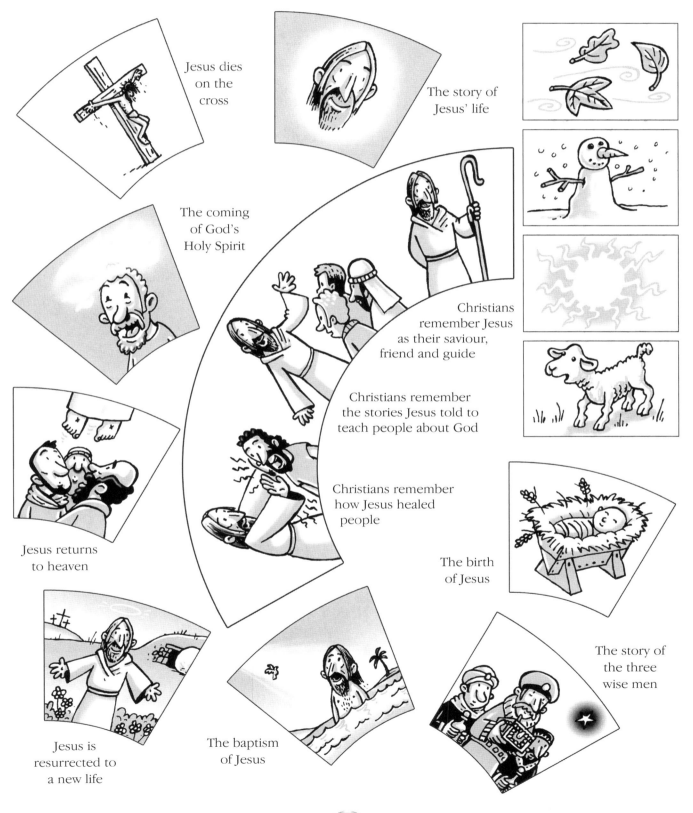

Jesus dies on the cross

The story of Jesus' life

The coming of God's Holy Spirit

Christians remember Jesus as their saviour, friend and guide

Christians remember the stories Jesus told to teach people about God

Christians remember how Jesus healed people

Jesus returns to heaven

The birth of Jesus

Jesus is resurrected to a new life

The baptism of Jesus

The story of the three wise men

www.barnabasinschools.org.uk

Reproduced with permission from *Living in Church* published by BRF 2006 (1 84101 399 4)

The Christian year reference sheet

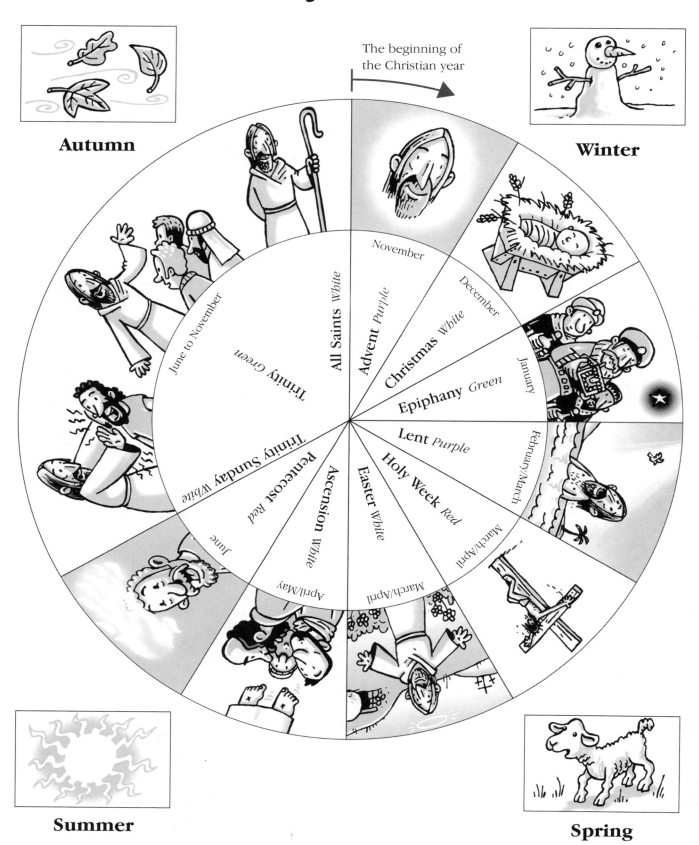

The beginning of the Christian year

Autumn

Winter

Summer

Spring

All Saints *White*

Advent *Purple*

Christmas *White*

Epiphany *Green*

Lent *Purple*

Holy Week *Red*

Easter *White*

Ascension *White*

Pentecost *Red*

Trinity Sunday *White*

Trinity *Green*

June to November

November

December

January

February/March

March/April

March/April

April/May

June

Religious language jargon buster

The Christian community has developed a language of technical terms over a 2000-year period. The glossary of terms below is intended to be used as a simple guide so that the language of the church can be communicated clearly to children without misunderstanding. *A Basic Church Dictionary* by Tony Meakin (Canterbury Press, 1990) is highly recommended for a more in-depth study.

General terms

Bible:	The holy book of the Christian faith containing the scriptures of the Old Testament and the New Testament.
Bishop:	A senior clergyman, appointed to oversee the spiritual direction of a diocese (see below).
Catholic:	A collective term for all Christian denominations, forming the universal church of Christ.
Church:	People belonging to the Christian community.
Church of England:	The Established Church (also known as the Anglican Church).
Churchwarden:	An official, appointed by the Bishop, who represents the interests of the parish or church.
Clergy:	See Minister.
Congregation:	A collective term for those who come to worship.
Denominations:	Different traditions of the worldwide Christian faith.
Diocese:	The circuit or extent of a Bishop's jurisdiction, encompassing a number of parishes.

Lay:	Those not ordained (see below) who carry out duties in the church.
Minister:	Someone who has been chosen, trained and given responsibility to lead a congregation.
Mission:	The sending out of people from the Christian community to show and share the love of God.
Ordained:	The recognized status of a minister (see above) trained to conduct a number of sacred duties such as celebrating Holy Communion, pronouncing God's forgiveness of sins, giving blessings and conducting a marriage ceremony.
Parish:	The geographic area of land for which a minister of the Established Church is responsible.
Parish church:	The church of that parish.
Pastor:	Title for a minister (see above)
Priest:	Title for a minister (see above)
Reverend:	Title for a minister (see above)
Vicar:	Title for a minister (see above)

Architectural terms

Altar:	The Communion table (traditionally made of stone).
Baptistry:	A place where people are symbolically washed clean by full immersion during a baptism.
Church building:	A building used for worship by the Christian community.
Chancel:	Area, originally designed for a choir, built on the east end of the main part of the church (nave) and closed off with a rood screen to celebrate Holy Communion.

Communion table: Table used to celebrate Holy Communion.

Crucifix: A depiction of Christ dying on the cross.

Font: A stone or wooden bowl on a stand, used for symbolic washing during a baptism (often found near the door of the church).

Lectern: A stand used to hold the Bible.

Nave: The main body of the church, where the congregation sits.

Pew: A fixed bench used as a seat during worship.

Pulpit: A raised structure used for preaching.

Rood screen: A wooden or stone screen dividing the nave and chancel, originally made to support a crucifixion scene. ('Rood' is an old English word meaning cross.)

Terms used during worship

Baptism: A ceremonial rite to mark a believer's entry into the Christian family.

Committal: The ceremony of placing a coffin in a grave, crematorium furnace or the sea.

Confirmation: A ceremonial rite to mark a believer's full admission to the Christian faith, confirming the promises made at baptism.

Christmas: The festival celebrating the birth of Jesus.

Creed: A summary of what Christians believe about God.

Crucifer: Person who carries a cross at the head of a procession.

Easter: The festival celebrating the death and resurrection of Jesus.

Eucharist: See Holy Communion.

Funeral: A ceremony to celebrate the life of a person who has died. A funeral is normally followed by a committal (see above).

Godparents: Those who promise to pray for and encourage the baptized person to follow Christ in their life.

Holy: Set apart (anything that expresses God, or is set apart to use for God).

Holy Communion: The symbolic sharing of bread and wine to represent the meal that Jesus ate with his friends on the night before he died.

Icon: A religious picture intended to help people pray.

Incarnation: The belief that God became a human being in the birth of Jesus.

Incense: A substance looking like coarse sand, which, when sprinkled on burning charcoal, gives off clouds of sweet-smelling smoke.

Lord's Supper: See Holy Communion.

Love: The nature of God, expressing pleasure in and affection for one another.

Mass: See Holy Communion.

Repent: To regret a thought or action and choose a new way; to turn back to God.

Resurrection: Being restored to life after death.

Robes: Vestments.

Sacred: Holy (see above): something that has been dedicated to God.

Server: Person who assists during a service.

Sharing the peace: A ritual during an act of worship, expressing our forgiveness of others, and being forgiven ourselves, for acts of wrongdoing that have divided us from other people and from God.

Thurible: The container for the burning charcoal and incense. It is usually suspended at the end of three chains so that it can be swung and also opened easily.

Vestments: Religious robes that express something symbolically in worship.

Worship: The adoration (love) of God, for all that God is and does.

Wedding: A ceremony to celebrate a lifelong faithful partnership of a man and woman in marriage.

Who's who in the Godhead

God: A description, not a name, used to refer to the one holy creative spirit, outside time, who has made everything in the universe.

The Trinity: An explanation of how we can know God in three special ways: as God the Father and creator of the universe; as Jesus the Son of God who lived 2000 years ago in Galilee and whose life is recorded in the four Gospels; and as the Holy Spirit of God who can be experienced as a guide and helper in the Christian life. Christians uphold the first of the Ten Commandments that there is only one God, but experience God in three unique ways. In the same way, we may experience the same person as a father, as a son and as a brother, in the knowledge that they are not three separate people, but one person.

Titles and names of Jesus

Jesus: A popular first name among Jewish men, full of spiritual significance. Jesus is a Greek form of the Hebrew name Joshua, meaning 'the Lord God is my help' or 'the Lord God rescues'. Thus even the name, Jesus, is a statement of faith.

Jesus of Nazareth: People with the same name were often called after the town where they had grown up. Nazareth, in northern Israel, was where Jesus grew up.

Son of God: A title denoting that, in the person of Jesus, God came to us in human form.

Lord: A powerful title of reverence and worship expressing the belief in Jesus' God-given authority.

Rabbi: A Jewish term of respect for a teacher.

Messiah: A Hebrew title used by the Jewish people for the long-expected saviour who would be sent by God to rescue them from political oppression. By his death and resurrection, Jesus demonstrated that his mission was to rescue us not from political oppression, but from spiritual death.

Christ: From the Greek word *khristos*, meaning 'God's anointed one'. This term refers to the image of anointing a king. The title means the same as Messiah. Eventually the title 'Christ' was joined to Jesus to create a statement of faith: Jesus the Christ or simply Jesus Christ.

Son of Man: A term that Jesus liked to use for himself. It reminded his followers that, although he shared divinity with God, by birth he was also fully human.

Emmanuel: The term given by the angel Gabriel to the baby Jesus, meaning 'God with us'.

Lamb of God: A title with Jewish religious roots, referring to the Old Testament practice of sacrificing a lamb to deal with the guilt and wrongdoing of people. Christians believe that Jesus is the once-for-all sacrifice for the wrongdoing of the whole world. The symbolic image of Jesus as the Lamb of God can be seen in many churches (and on some school uniforms).

Some New Testament biblical characters

Mary: The mother of Jesus. In some traditions called St Mary, the Blessed Virgin Mary, or Mary, the mother of God (Jesus). In many church traditions, Mary is greatly respected.

Joseph: A carpenter engaged to Mary at the time when she became pregnant through the Holy Spirit. Joseph married Mary and took on the role of Jesus' earthly father. Sometimes called St Joseph, with Mary and Jesus Joseph is part of 'the holy family'.

Disciples: People who follow Jesus, particularly his twelve closest friends: Peter, John, Andrew, James, Philip, Bartholomew, Thomas, Matthew, James, Thaddeus, Simon and Judas Iscariot. All but Judas Iscariot (who betrayed Jesus) are often referred to as saints.

Apostles: Someone sent to preach the gospel, especially the twelve disciples (see above) and others in the New Testament, such as St Paul (see below).

Pilate: The name of a historically recorded civic governor in charge of Roman power over Jerusalem. He is recorded in the Bible as the one responsible for the miscarriage of justice when he condemned Jesus to be executed on the cross.

Paul: Paul, whose original Jewish name was Saul, started out as the sworn enemy of the early Christians, organizing a reign of terror that saw the execution of many of the first followers of Jesus. He changed his name to Paul when he was converted to Christianity after experiencing a vision of the risen Christ, and became one of the most influential people in the early development of Christianity. Paul is often referred to as St Paul.

Gospel writers: Matthew, Mark, Luke and John. Their writings form the first five books of the New Testament (the book of Acts was written by Luke). They are often referred to as saints.